LIFE-GIVING
LEADERSHIP

JACK W. HAYFORD

NELSON REFERENCE & ELECTRONIC
A Division of Thomas Nelson Publishers
www.thomasnelson.com

Spirit-Filled Life® Study Guide: Life-Giving Leadership

Copyright © 2004 by Jack W. Hayford

Printed in Nashville, Tennessee, by Thomas Nelson, Inc.

Unless otherwise indicated, all Scripture quotations are from the New King James Version, copyright © 1979, 1980, 1982, 1990 by Thomas Nelson, Inc.

Library of Congress Cataloging-in-Publication Data

Hayford, Jack W.
  Life-giving leadership / Jack W. Hayford
    p. cm. -- (Spirit-filled life study guide)
  ISBN 0-7852-4988-5 (trade paper)
1. Christian leadership. I. Title
  BV652.1.H37 2004
  253--dc22

                              2004020350

Printed in the United States of America

            1 2 3 4 5 6 7—09 08 07 06 05 04

CONTENTS

INTRODUCTION

A s you move forward in your desire to be a servant of God, you will hear Him calling you to new dimensions of faith—and that may include a call to leadership. This call is different than the initial call to faith for your salvation or for personal needs and growth. It is an invitation to exercise those steps of faith needful to serve others, to lead in various aspects of church work, and to impact the darkness with the light of the gospel. This may be to serve as a Sunday school or Bible study teacher, to lead an outreach ministry of your church or to fulfill a servant-leader role within your church, such as deacon or elder.

Life-Giving Leadership will help you develop sensitivity to the Holy Spirit as God guides you into fruitful leadership ministry. This study will:

☑ Help you to fully experience God's purpose for your life

☑ Inspire you to serve with joy in obedience to His call

☑ Show the value of Spirit-formed character and openness with others

☑ Encourage you to release spiritual gifts in those you lead

☑ Inspire you to intercede in prayer, igniting evangelism and revival

☑ Invite you to believe God for miracles to be manifested among the people

☑ Encourage you to embrace God-given visions and dreams— now and in your future

God is calling for leaders today. He is asking, *"Whom shall I send, and who will go for Us?"* (Is. 6:8). May we hear His call and respond with excellence of heart.

"WHO ME?"

Lesson 1

THE BIG IDEA

"Who am I, that God could use me?" If you have ever said that, you are not alone! Come and discover the same power-packed truth that many biblical leaders experienced: *God has significant purpose for you.*

PEOPLE WHO MAKE A DIFFERENCE

The Word of God makes clear that it is God's will to use individuals and to make them of enormous significance. In this lesson, you will be encouraged to receive God's call to life-giving leadership as you study biblical leaders in adverse circumstances who found great purpose through God's call on their lives.

All of these leaders are renowned by reason of the record of their experience in Scripture and of how the Lord used them. Our tendency is to respond, "Yes, but those people are special. Look at what they did. Who am I, in comparison to them?" It is important to realize that many biblical leaders pondered their insignificance in the face of God's call. *Such thinking does not disqualify us from service; it moves God to reveal His sufficiency if we will allow Him.*

MOSES

In the third chapter of Exodus, the Lord met Moses, a stuttering shepherd who felt that he had missed his moment in life. Years before, Moses had attempted to achieve what he thought God wanted him to do, and because of that, was exiled in Egypt.

What did Moses try to accomplish in his own strength, and what happened as a result? (Acts 7:22–29; see also Ex. 2:11–15)

◇ The whole story of God's call for Moses to deliver Israel is found in Exodus 3:1—4:17. What did God want Moses to do? (3:10)

◈ What did Moses first say when God called him to do a work for Him? (3:11)

_____

_____

◈ How did God respond to Moses' lack of confidence? (3:14)

_____

_____

What a difference a word makes! God rearranged the order of Moses' words, answering Moses' question, "Who am I?" with "I AM WHO I AM" (the self-existent One). When God promised Moses that He would be with him, He was affirming that He would be a protector and sustainer of His people.

KINGDOM EXTRA

Revealing His divine name as "I AM WHO I AM," God declares His character and attributes, reinforcing that the issue is not who Moses is, but Who is with him. This name is related to the Hebrew verb meaning "to be," and so implies the absolute existence of God. The Hebrew here is also the source of the English, "Yahweh," "Jehovah," or "Lord."

Let's look again at Moses' initial reluctance to respond to God's call to spiritual leadership. From the Book of Exodus, list the different excuses Moses gave and the ways God responded to them.

Moses' Excuse	God's Response
Exodus 3:11, 12	
Exodus 3:13, 14	
Exodus 4:1–9	
Exodus 4:10–12	
Exodus 4:13–17	

God had assured Moses that He would be with him to enable him to succeed in the great task to which he was called. With that assurance, Moses set out to do what God had commanded him to do (Ex. 4:20).

◊ When Moses was obedient to God's call, how did the people initially respond? (Ex. 4:31)

We all know the end of the story. The Lord called Moses to withstand the temporal world system, the works of darkness and the powers of hell. Because Moses was obedient to His call, God brought about the deliverance of a nation (Acts 7:36; Ex.14). The lesson learned from Moses is clear: *Experiencing God's sufficiency in the face of our insufficiency will revolutionize our ability to become leaders.*

FAITH ALIVE

Often the Lord says to the person who thinks, *I've missed my moment,* "No matter what's happened in the past, you're the person I've chosen to use." Have you ever felt "left out" in ministry or ministered to someone who felt that way? How can Moses' story encourage the person who feels they have little to offer?

DAVID

"Who am I?" Many years after Moses' time, David spoke those same words. We know David as the king of Israel, successful in leadership and in worship. Yet, David came from humble beginnings.

◊ What did David say of himself in 2 Samuel 7:18?

◊ Read the account of how David was chosen to be king in 1 Samuel 16:1–13. What do you think caused him to feel, "Who am I?"

This former shepherd boy, who once was ignored by his family, said *yes* to his God. At the end of his life, David as king had led Israel well, despite his failures. He had served God faithfully by composing many of the beloved Psalms we read today.

ELIJAH

God worked many miracles through Elijah. He prayed, and his prayer changed the climate of an entire nation—and changed its destiny.

◇ James 5:17, 18 describes a powerful miracle that God worked through Elijah's prayer. What was the miracle?

_____

◇ Was Elijah "better" than we are? Use the description of Elijah's nature from verse 17 in your answer.

_____

◇ What happened when Elijah thought he was the only one in the country who was following God? (1 Kin. 19:10–12)

_____

◇ What encouragement does it give us to know that God revealed His presence in the face of Elijah's doubts?

_____

TAKING THE NEXT STEP

All these leaders had something in common. They had doubts, fears, and inadequacies, but God met them where they were. Some were slow to respond, but in the end, they all stepped past their limitation and obeyed God's call to serve. They realized that the issue isn't WHO WE ARE; the issue is WHO GOD IS. They trusted in God, realizing His power far surpassed their own personal strength or wisdom, and that this power was readily available to them.

Mary, the mother of Jesus, is an example of a person who learned this truth. When the angel came to her and told her that she was going to birth the Son of God, she responded with, "How can this be?" (Luke 1:34). The angel's answer was very clear. The miraculous entry of God's Redeemer through her was going to happen when the Holy Spirit's power came upon her.

◇ Turn to Luke 1:35. What did the angel tell Mary?

_____

_____

◇ What was Mary's response to the coming miracle? (v. 38)

_____

_____

◇ Turn to 2 Corinthians 4:7. This passage expresses how even fragile human beings can be instruments of God's power. How is this power described?

_____

_____

◇ Are we sufficient in ourselves to do God's work? Who makes us to be significant ministers of the gospel? (2 Cor. 3:5, 6)

_____

_____

The power of God happens when God can find the person who will say, "Lord, my words say *who am I*, but Your words speak to me about Your sufficiency. I will do what You want me to do."

FAITH ALIVE

◇ Write down any reluctance you may be struggling with that would hinder you from experiencing the purpose of God in your life. Then list the steps you plan to take in dealing with your issues of reluctance.

_____

_____

◈ If you wish, share this with a trusted friend. As you seek to replace your insufficiency with God's sufficiency, ask for agreement in prayer that you may learn to stop focusing on your limitations and realize who God is.

_____

_____

GOD'S GREAT PURPOSE

As you look beyond your limitations to God's sufficiency, you will find He has significant purpose for your life.

◈ What has God prepared for those who love Him? (1 Cor. 2:9)

_____

◈ What kinds of plans does God have for you? (Jer. 29:11)

_____

◈ What are you to do in order to see God's "great and mighty things"? (Jer. 33:3)

_____

◈ Write out Romans 8:28, focusing on the phrase, "called according to His purpose."

_____

◈ Using the Word Wealth definition as a starting point, write your definition of the word "purpose."

_____

WORD WEALTH

Purpose, _prothesis_ (Rom. 8:28). From _pro_, "before," and _thesis_, "a place," thus "a setting forth. The word suggests a deliberate plan, a proposition, an advance plan, an intention, a design. Of twelve occurrences in the New Testament, *prothesis* is used four times for the Levitical showbread (literally "the bread of setting before"). Most of the other usages point to God's eternal purposes relating to salvation. Our personal salvation was not only well planned but demonstrates God's abiding faithfulness as He awaits the consummation of His great plan for His church.

FAITH ALIVE

How can understanding God's sufficiency help you find your purpose in Him?

PURPOSE THROUGH PARTNERSHIP

Your purpose in God's design is not an automatically programmed life process that involves no particular response on your part—as though you just put your wheels down and let a "heavenly wind" move you where you are to go! Rather, Scripture summons you to *partner* with the living God to see the kingdom of God advanced in you and through you. This involves accepting divinely appointed limits on His side of the partnership, as well as on your side. Coming to accept those limits is a pivotal issue in learning the Lord's way to see your own personal purpose realized.

1. God's side of the partnership: God's sovereign limit is that *He wills to work through human agency to advance His purposes.*

◇ For what purpose did Jesus show Himself to Paul? (Acts 26:16)

_____

_____

◇ Turn to the Lord's Prayer in Matthew 6:9–13. How are we to pray regarding His will? (v. 10)

_____

_____

◇ What does that prayer tell you about God's desire to partner with you to see His kingdom rule established in the spiritual realm?

_____

_____

12

What God wills on the heaven side of things will be released in earth by the invitation of human agents. Those people who say, "Lord, I want Your rule in my life" are the ones that are going to cooperate with God's purpose.

2. Our side of the partnership: Our sovereignly designed limits are that *we are to obey and walk within the boundaries of His Word and depend upon His Spirit.*

◇ Turn to Luke 4:1–10. Here, Jesus gave us the example of choosing to submit to the Word of God. How do verses 4, 8, and 12 show that Jesus stayed within the limits of God's Word?

_____

_____

_____

◇ In order for Timothy to be effective in ministry, what did Paul counsel Timothy to do? (1 Tim. 4:13, 14; 2 Tim. 2:15)

_____

_____

_____

◇ What did Paul depend on when he preached? (1 Cor. 2:4, 5, 13)

_____

_____

Our responsibility is to live within the boundaries of His Word, to be led by His Spirit, and to function in partnership with Him. Then we can see our highest purpose realized for His eternal glory.

YOUR ROLE IN HIS PURPOSE

Who are you? You are a son, a daughter of the most high God. Who is God? He is God, the all-sufficient, self-existent One, who has given you purpose of huge significance. God wants us to partner with Him so that His purpose might be advanced through us. This will happen as we learn—in the joy of His presence and in the adequacy of His provision—to be His hand reaching and touching people for what He wills to bring about.

FAITH ALIVE

◇ What do you feel is God's purpose for your life?

_____

_____

◇ Are there certain ministries yet unrealized in your life? What are they?

_____

_____

◇ Do you see that there could be expanding ministry possibilities of seeing God's purposes realized through you as you partner with Him?

_____

_____

_____

OBEY GOD'S CALL
Lesson 2

THE BIG IDEA

How does God "call" people into His service today? The answer is not mysterious or nebulous. Discover the joy of hearing and obeying God's call in your life.

YOUR UNIQUE CALL

◇ Have you sensed an inward drawing to follow God at a new level?

_____

_____

◇ Have you have been moved by the hopeless plight of unevangelized people?

_____

_____

◇ Has someone told you they see leadership potential in you?

_____

_____

◇ Have you responded to a public appeal to serve God?

_____

_____

◇ Do you believe that God has sovereignly spoken to you about His call on your life?

_____

_____

_____

God's call to leadership comes in various ways, and it summons all kinds of people for different types of service. In whatever manner God communicates His call to you, when you obey it, you will experience fulfillment as you impact people for Christ.

CALLED, NOT DRIVEN

True spiritual leaders do not serve God out of a sense of compulsion. Rather, they are drawn to lead by God's Spirit. In his book *Transforming Leadership*, Leighton Ford writes, "Genuine leaders operate out of a sense of calling, not a sense of drivenness."[1] He adds, "The writer George MacDonald has said . . . that real Christian leaders are people who are moved at God's pace and in God's time to God's place, not because they fancy themselves there, but because they are drawn."[2]

◈ What do you think is the difference between being *driven* to serve and *drawn* to serve God?

Let's consider what your call to serve God means by studying the biblical definition of "call." Galatians 1:6 says that God "called you in the grace of Christ."

WORD WEALTH

Called, *kaleo* (Gal. 1:6). From the root *kal*, the source of the English words "call" and "clamor." The word is used to invite or to summon, and is especially used of God's call to participate in the blessings of the kingdom.

◈ What is the difference between the call of God and a demand?

KINGDOM EXTRA

For in-depth study, examine the Scriptures following each definition section of "call" taken from *The Analytical Greek Lexicon: New Testament* (New York: Harper and Brothers Publishers), 211.

Call, *kaleo*: to call, or call to (John 10:3); to call into one's presence, send for a person (Matt. 2:7); to summon (Matt. 2:15, Matt. 25:14); to invite (Matt. 22:9); to call to the performance of a certain thing (Matt. 9:13; Heb. 11:8); to call to a participation in the privileges of the gospel (Rom. 8:30, 9:24; 1 Cor. 1:9, 7:18); to call to an office of dignity (Heb. 5:4).

FAITH ALIVE

◇ How would you describe your calling at this time?

_____

_____

◇ Are there things yet to be realized in your call? List some of them here.

_____

_____

_____

THE CALL TO REPENTANCE

God desires all "to be saved and come to the knowledge of the truth" (1 Tim. 2:4); yet only a few respond (Matt. 7:13, 14; 22:14).

Read the following verses and note the nature of the God's call and who is being called.

Mark 2:17 _____

_____

Acts 2:39 _____

_____

FAITH ALIVE

Everyone who comes to Christ is like a "diamond in the rough." A diamond does not reflect its true beauty until it has been removed from the rough soil in which it was found and is polished in the hands of a skilled gemologist, mounted in gold or silver, and displayed for all to see. Even so it is with us when we come to Christ. Through the process of discipleship, He cleanses us, polishes us, and sets us as lights in the world, reflectors of His splendor, and servants of the Most High God.

◇ Is there an area in your life that represents a diamond in the rough?

_____

_____

◇ List steps you can take to submit to Christ's discipleship so that He can "polish" this area in your life.

_____

_____

_____

_____

THE CALL TO DISCIPLESHIP

With just two powerful words, "Follow Me," Jesus called twelve men to be His disciples. So impacted were these Twelve that they left what they were doing to obey Him. No longer would they independently decide the direction of their lives. Instead, they would follow where He led and be changed from the inside out.

Mark 3:14, 15 describes it this way: "Then He appointed twelve, that they might be with Him and that He might send them out to preach, and to have power to heal sicknesses and to cast out demons." The Greek verb "appointed" means "to make someone into something." And make them into something is exactly what God did! Out of these followers (except for Judas Iscariot) came apostles who delivered God's Word and accomplished His kingdom work in the founding of the church.

Jesus' initial call to His disciples is described in Matthew 4:18–22, Mark 1:16–20, Luke 5:2–11, and John 1:40–42. Read each of these accounts and comment on leadership principles that can be extracted from these verses.

1. Jesus used terms familiar to the fishermen and met them on their own familiar territory (Luke 5:4, 10; Matt. 4:18, 19).

(It is interesting to note that the word Jesus used for "catch men" in Luke 5:10 means "to capture alive." Its tense suggests continuous action. From now on Peter and the others are called to continuously capture people alive for the kingdom of God.)

Leadership principle learned:

2. Sometimes a seemingly "insignificant" person brings some-one to Jesus who will become better known or have a "big-ger ministry" than his (Andrew brought Peter to Jesus, John 1:40–42).

Leadership principle learned:

3. Jesus understood the importance of relationship.
    A. He called two sets of brothers (Matt. 4:18, 21).
    B. Some of the disciples-to-be already knew each other; James and John were fishing partners with Simon Peter (Luke 5:10).
    C. Jesus invested Himself into His disciples as He spent time mentoring them.

Leadership principle learned:

4. Heeding Jesus' call involves total commitment to Him (Mark 1:18, 20; Luke 5:11). Jesus' disciples were willing to leave all behind.

Leadership principle learned:

Disciples of Jesus Christ are not just passive followers. Check out the full meaning of "disciples" from the Word Wealth definition.

WORD WEALTH

Disciples, *mathetes* (Matt. 10:1). From the verb *manthano*, "to learn," whose root *math* suggests thought with effort put forth. A disciple is a learner, one who follows both the teaching and the teacher. The word is used first of the Twelve and later of Christians generally.

◇ What does the Greek root word "math" mean and what is its connection to discipleship?

_____

_____

◇ Is discipleship a mental exercise only, or does it involve the whole person? Why?

_____

_____

_____

◇ What is the purpose of discipleship?

_____

_____

The call to discipleship brought dramatic changes to Jesus' followers. As He taught them the principles of the kingdom of God, their relationship with God changed. God, who had been known to them as the great Creator and the God of their fathers, now became known to them as their heavenly Father. Their relationship with others changed as the teachings of Jesus cleansed them from prejudice. Their worldview changed when they realized they were to take the gospel to the world. Even their professions changed as they left their nets to become "fishers of men," or left the tax table to receive a spiritual harvest for God's kingdom.

Nothing would ever be the same for these disciples. Little did they realize what great and wonderful things lay in store for them because of their obedience to the call to serve God. Patiently, Jesus taught them about His kingdom. As they watched Him minister to the people, they learned that His was a kingdom built upon compassion, forgiveness, and love. After they had grown in their understanding of His ways, He empowered them by His Spirit to go and call others to follow Him. They learned that in His name and by the authority of His Word they had power to minister to others just as they had seen Him do.

◇ How did the disciples change?

_____

_____

◇ Contrast what the disciples gained with what they lost through their decision to follow Christ wholeheartedly. Which lifestyle was the most fulfilling? Why?

_____

_____

FAITH ALIVE

Like the Twelve, you too have heard Jesus' call to discipleship. As you respond to His call, there are, no doubt, many changes taking place in your life.

◇ How has your relationship with Jesus as His disciple changed you? (Consider your relationship with God and with others, your worldview, and your occupation.)

_____

_____

◇ How can you help or encourage others to experience similar blessings of discipleship?

_____

_____

THE CALL TO SERVE

In Scripture we see that the methods God uses to call His leaders varies. Also, how people respond to His call varies. Such is the way of God—He does not offer the same "cookie cutter" call to everyone, but designs and calls each person individually.

◇ Take a look at different individuals who received God's call to leadership. Write what God called them to do and how they responded.

Abram/Abraham (Gen. 12:1–5) _____

_____

Isaiah (Is. 6:1–8) _____

_____

Saul of Tarsus (Acts 9:1–20) _____

_____

Barnabas and Saul (Acts 13:2–4) _____

Aaron (Heb. 5:4; see also Ex. 28:1) _____

_____

_____

AN UNLIKELY LEADER

Let's take a closer look at Saul of Tarsus, dreaded persecutor of the church, later to become Paul the apostle.

◇ What was Paul's background before meeting Christ? (Acts 8:1–3; Phil. 3:5, 6)

_____

_____

◇ What did Paul say of his calling? (Rom. 1:1)

_____

_____

◇ Describe Paul's dramatic conversion. (Acts 9:1–9)

_____

_____

◇ How did Paul respond to God's voice? (Acts 9:6)

_____

_____

◇ Ananias was the one God called to minister to Saul, who had been blinded by the light of God's glory. Was Ananias afraid to go? (Acts 9:10–14)

_____

_____

◇ What did God tell Ananias about this new convert? (Acts 9:15, 16)

_____

_____

◇ What happened when Ananias finally went to pray for Saul? (Acts 9:17–19)

_____

_____

_____

◈ Imagine yourself in Ananias' sandals. What do you think would have happened if he hadn't obeyed God's call to go to Saul?

◈ After his conversion, what was Paul's attitude regarding his background and status? (Phil. 3:7, 8)

Saul of Tarsus was a zealous persecutor of the church when he received the call of God. Before his conversion, he was greatly feared by the Christians because he sought to destroy them—all in the name of God—he thought.

Sometimes the call of God comes to the most unexpected persons, in the most unexpected ways. If God chooses to do so, He will call the educated or the uneducated, the addict or criminal, the professional or unprofessional. Who would have thought that Saul of Tarsus, the persecutor, would become a chosen vessel of the Lord? As His followers, we are to let God be God, and to let Him choose whom He will. Our responsibility is simply to respond when He calls.

◈ What hope does Saul's conversion give you and the people you lead?

GOD'S CALL TO YOU

God needs leaders today. He is asking some to leave familiar surroundings, areas of comfort, and familiar routines. Others are called to stay in the place where they are already planted—in their church home or community. Wherever His call takes us, we will experience the blessed benefits of His redemptive purposes.

When Jesus said to Matthew the tax collector, "Follow Me," Matthew arose and followed Him (Matt. 9:9). When Jesus said, "Follow Me" to a group of fishermen, they also immediately responded by leaving their nets and following Him (Matt. 4:18–22). May we hear Him say, "Whom shall I send, and who will go for Us?" (Is. 6:8). And may those of us whom God calls to spiritual leadership today be as prompt in our response!

FAITH ALIVE

Are you hesitant to trust the Lord with all your heart when it comes to leaving your comfort zone? Do you fear He will lead you to a place less fulfilling than the one you're already headed toward? Or do you feel that because you were not raised in a Christian home with proper religious training, you could never fulfill God's call to leadership in ministry?

Take a moment to reflect on Saul's background, his call, and his immediate response to the call. Then consider the position of spiritual leadership you sense God calling you to. Write a note to the Lord expressing your heart and asking for His help where you may be struggling to respond to His call.

_____

_____

_____

_____

_____

_____

_____

_____

_____

_____

_____

_____

_____

_____

_____

_____

_____

_____

_____

SERVE WITH JOY
Lesson 3

THE BIG IDEA

The measure for success in leadership is not in how we rule, but in how we serve. Find the joy in serving—God's way.

GREATNESS BEGINS WITH SERVING

Marjorie was a young woman preparing for ministry at L.I.F.E. Bible College. One day as she rushed through a school hall, she spotted a broom lying across a busy entryway. In their haste to get to their classes, the other students were stepping over the broom. "I wonder how that broom got there. I'll move it so no one stumbles," thought Marjorie, tucking it away in a corner. Just then, a woman who had been watching from behind a newspaper sprung towards Marjorie. This person was Aimee Semple McPherson, the founder of the college. Placing her hand on Marjorie's arm, this great woman of God said, "I put that broom there because I was looking for a leader who would serve others. You will do great things for Christ."

That power-packed prophetic word became a reality in Marjorie's life. She and her husband became missionaries, traveling throughout South and Central America to proclaim the Good News of Jesus Christ. Their grandchildren still preach the gospel today. Aimee McPherson, in very creative fashion, found a servant for Christ!

FAITH ALIVE

◈ What did Marjorie learn that prepared her for service to Christ? How can you apply that to your life?

_____

_____

◇ Before launching into this study, ask the Holy Spirit to show you how servanthood fits into the process of forming a leader.

_____

_____

THE DEPTH OF SERVANTHOOD

Imagine a person choosing to become an ant. That doesn't even begin to explain the magnitude of the change that took place when Jesus left heaven and became human. In His preincarnate glory, Jesus was equal with the Father and was the Creator of the world (John 1:1–3). In His Incarnation, He came down from His glory and was born as a human being (John 1:14); He humbled Himself to serve.

Here are just a few examples of how Jesus served others. Describe the humility of Christ demonstrated in each verse:

John 13:5–16
_____

Luke 2:7
_____

Matthew 11:29
_____

◇ What did Jesus say His purpose was? (Mark 10:45)

_____

_____

A missionary to a third-world country brought a delegation of believers to the United States to attend a convention. One day she took the group to a modern supermarket, and as they passed through the produce area, one of the foreign pastors started weeping. Concerned, the lady missionary asked what was wrong. He responded, "Only now am I realizing how many comforts you and your family left behind in order to take the gospel to our country."

It is true that every missionary who leaves the comforts of home, family, and friends to take the gospel to other lands pays a great price. But it cannot begin to compare with the great price Christ paid by leaving heaven to come to earth to redeem humankind.

FAITH ALIVE

Meditate on Jesus' willingness to exit heaven to serve on earth. In your quiet time, thank God for His gift of humility demonstrated through His Son.

THE GREATNESS OF SERVANTHOOD

The apostle Paul appealed to believers to serve one another in humility by following Christ's example. Turn to Philippians 2:3–11.

◇ Whose interests are you to look out for in addition to your own? (v. 4)

_____

_____

◇ Whose example of service are we to follow? (v. 5)

_____

_____

◇ Write out the fantastic message of verses 6, 7. (In a moment you will study this passage in more detail.)

_____

_____

◇ Who is the supreme example of humility? Why? (v. 8)

_____

_____

◇ What was the ultimate result of Jesus' willing obedience to go to the Cross? (vv. 9–11)

_____

_____

Now, turn again to verses 6–9 to explore five wonderful truths. After each truth, write the significance of this truth to your faith.

1. "Being in the form of God. . ." This phrase means that the essence of Jesus Christ is the very same as that of the

Father, for He is Himself God. This is important when we compare who He is with His mission on earth.

◇ What this truth means to me:

_____

_____

2. ". . . did not consider it robbery to be equal with God. . ." Another way to explain this would be "something to be held on to in order to be equal." This references the fact that Jesus saw His being God as something to be given away, not selfishly grasped. He willingly became a human being on our behalf, relinquishing His glory though retaining His deity.

◇ What this truth means to me:

_____

_____

3. ". . . made Himself of no reputation. . ." comes from the Greek word *ekenesen*, which means to divest one's self of one's prerogatives, to abase one's self, to empty one's self of one's privileges. It is important to realize that Jesus emptied Himself of the glories attendant to His deity, but not of deity itself.

◇ What this truth means to me:

_____

_____

4. ". . . He humbled Himself. . ." Jesus didn't flaunt, prove, or push through self-advancement the fullness of all God had placed in Him. Jesus' complete absence of any need to "clutch" for power or attention is manifest humility. It is the royal Spirit that the King of heaven Himself displayed in servantlike graciousness.

◇ What this truth means to me:

_____

_____

5. "God also has highly exalted Him. . ." Just as Christ's humility received ultimate exaltation, so our call to "humble

yourselves in the sight of the Lord, [that] He will lift [us] up" points to the way for the rise of God's highest purpose in each of us (James 4:10). Humbling ourselves opens us up to increased grace (James 4:6; 1 Pet. 5:5), and childlikeness is the doorway to the dynamism of "kingdom come" in our life and service (Matt. 18:4).

◈ What this truth means to me:

_____

_____

In his book, *Descending into Greatness*, Bill Hybels comments on the humility described in Philippians 2. "Simply stated, the message of Philippians is this: If you want to be truly great, then the direction you must go is down. You must descend into greatness. At the heart of this paradox is still another paradox: Greatness is not a measure of self-will, but rather self-abandonment. The more you lose, the more you gain." [3]

THE HUMILITY OF SERVANTHOOD

◈ Jesus' own disciples wrestled with the matter of greatness vs. serving. They got to the point where they asked Jesus outright who would be the greatest in the kingdom of heaven (Matt. 18:1). How did He respond to their question? (vv. 2–4)

_____

_____

When Jesus told His disciples that greatness is defined by a person's willingness to be humble like a child, He was confronting the tendency of humankind to associate *authority* with an exercise of *dominance* over others. The dominion or authority in kingdom life God wants to reinstate in us is for victorious fruitful living and for the overthrow of hellish powers, not for gaining control of others or for serving our own interests. His call to childlike humility and a servant-like heart establishes the spirit and style by which the authority of the believer is to be exercised as a ministering agent of God's kingdom power. (See Matt. 19:14; Mark 10:14, 15; Luke 18:16, 17.)

To enhance understanding of what Jesus meant when He said, "Whoever humbles himself as this little child," let's look at the Word Wealth definition.

WORD WEALTH

Humbles, *tapeinoo* (Matt. 18:4). Literally, "to make low," used of a mountain in Luke 3:5. Metaphorically, the word means to debase, humble, lower oneself. It describes a person who is devoid of all arrogance and self-exaltation—a person who is willingly submitted to God and His will.

◇ Using this Word Wealth definition, describe in your own words a person who is humble.

_____

_____

◇ Read Luke 3:5, 6. When every mountain shall be made low and everything will be made straight, or right, what will be the result? (v. 6)

_____

_____

◇ What will happen when a person humbles himself? (1 Pet. 5:5)

_____

_____

FAITH ALIVE

Is humility synonymous with lack of self-esteem? Why or why not? How can people be humble without losing their authority to lead?

MOTIVATED TO SERVE

Servanthood is the time-tested prerequisite for trustworthy ministry. Since God's Word encourages loving service, we are wise to strive to become rising leaders who have right attitudes about serving others.

Let's look at some examples where those who would become leaders rendered personal service. Who was served and what kind of service was it?

Moses (Ex. 3:1)

_____

Joshua (Ex. 24:13; Josh. 1:1) _____

Elisha (2 Kin. 3:11) _____

David (1 Sam. 16:21; 17:32) _____

Jesus set the example for all who would follow Him in ministry. There was nothing self-serving about Him. His service was motivated by genuine love.

◇ What emotion did Jesus feel when He saw the weariness of the crowd? (Matt. 9:36)

_____

_____

◇ What does Matthew 11:28, 29 reveal about Jesus' concern for people?

_____

_____

◇ Why do we weep with those who weep and rejoice with those who rejoice? (Rom. 12:15)

_____

_____

◇ How closely does Jesus sympathize with us? (Heb. 4:15)

_____

_____

Love compassionately relates to the lost, the hurting, the needy, and the distressed. It moves more and more into the dimension of discipleship that discovers the compassion of Christ flowing through a person to care for and serve others.

FAITH ALIVE

What does Jesus' compassion speak to you about His call to care for others?

JOY IN SERVING

A woman was working in a very responsible position in a school that trained Christian leaders. When her health began to fail, she went to a clinic for an extensive physical examination. The findings of the examination were surprising. There was nothing physically wrong with the woman! It was determined that her problem was stress.

The doctor asked what it was that would bring such stress in her life. Her response was a surprise to herself as well as to the doctor. She told him she was not happy with the work she was doing, but because of circumstances that she felt were beyond her control, she had no choice but to serve. Though she served faithfully and efficiently, she did not tell anyone of the inward struggle she was having. As a result, the inner conflict was ruining her health.

It is important that we find the position of ministry that God has for us, and then serve wholeheartedly and willingly in that position. Instead of stress, we will experience joy in God's service.

◇ In the New Testament, Peter tells leaders *not* to serve God out of a sense of compulsion. What two *positive* attitudes are to be characteristic of our serving? (1 Pet. 5:2)

_____

_____

◇ What happens when a person serves because they feel "cornered" into doing it?

_____

_____

◇ In the Old Testament, David is an example of a person who served God willingly and wholeheartedly. God was pleased with David's attitude toward Him. How did God commend David? (1 Sam. 13:14)

_____

_____

_____

◇ David gave his son Solomon good advice not only for the future king, but also for all who serve God and lead others. What was this wise advice? (1 Chr. 28:9)

_____

_____

_____

FAITH ALIVE

Are you experiencing stress in heeding your call to ministry as a result of lack of joy or willingness to serve? Write down your thoughts about the situation; then pray and ask the Holy Spirit to reveal the root cause of your stress or dissatisfaction. As He reveals the truth to you, write down how you plan to deal with it.

◇ How has Jesus' willingness to humbly serve touched you?

_____

_____

_____

◇ How would you encourage someone else to be servant-hearted?

_____

_____

_____

CHARACTER QUALITIES THAT COUNT
Lesson 4

THE BIG IDEA

Moses was close to big-time burnout! From morning until sunset, he ministered to people practically all by himself. Then Moses received sound advice that revolutionized his leadership methods—*find leaders of good character to help you lead!* Putting this wise plan into action, Moses reduced his stress and exponentially increased the people's understanding of God. The process by which leaders mentor and grow other leaders is fruitful when we understand what kinds of character qualities God looks for in His leaders.

FIND POTENTIAL LEADERS

When Moses "did it all" the people *did* receive from God, but there were also three negative effects:

1. Moses was overworked.
2. The people did not receive justice quickly.
3. Potential leaders were deprived of the opportunity to use their talents.

However, when Moses selected and integrated leaders into his ministry, there came a multiplication of the understanding of God among the people. It is important that a spiritual leader likewise be on the lookout for new leadership to develop.

Let's begin this study by seeing what character qualifications were important to Moses as he selected leaders to assist him. Read Exodus 18:13–26.

◇ What was Moses' schedule like? (v. 13)

_____

_____

◇ What was the good work that Moses was doing? Was it vital to the survival of the nation of Israel? (vv. 15, 16)

◇ What was *not* good about the single-handed way Moses was carrying out his responsibilities? (vv. 17, 18)

◇ What advice did Moses' father-in-law give on how to administrate the work? (vv. 19–22)

◇ What four qualifications were these leaders to have? (v. 21)

◇ What was Moses to teach them? (v. 20)

◇ What was the result of the training of leaders? (vv. 23–26)

Look again at the qualities Moses' potential leaders needed to possess (v. 21). Using the scriptural cross-reference, write a short definition of each quality. Use a dictionary if necessary.

1. Capable (see Acts 6:3)
2. Fears God (see 2 Sam. 23:3)
3. Is truthful and trustworthy (see Ezek. 18:8)
4. Hates covetousness (see Deut. 16:19)

As a result of Moses' choice to delegate ministry, God's purposes were made known to more people. Very important in this process was selecting people with the right kind of leadership qualities. But how does one identify potential leaders? What kind of people should they be? What kind of character traits should they demonstrate?

IMPORTANT CHARACTER QUALITIES

The Bible gives character guidelines that are essential to a spiritual leader's personal and public life. These have to do with what the person *is*, not what he/she *achieves*. Most important is the condition of a leader's heart and spirit. Remember that God said David was a "man after My own heart" (Acts 13:22).

Why, then, do we study the character qualities that are important to leadership? Because many people in our culture today do not have a moral yardstick to measure integrity of conduct and they need to know what kinds of qualities the Holy Spirit will grow in them as they mature in their relationship with Christ.

Turn again to the sixth chapter of Acts. Here, the fledgling church was in desperate need of good leaders. The apostles were not able to pray and minister the Word because they were too busy with other duties overseeing a burgeoning congregation. They gave instructions to choose seven people having specific qualifications to serve in the church.

◇ According to Acts 6:3, what three things should be characteristic of a person who wants to be used by God?

_____

_____

If these qualities were essential then, it is also important for the Life-giving leader to encourage their development in others. This exercise is designed to help you study in depth each of these three qualities.

1. Good reputation: The Greek word for "good reputation" in Acts 6:3 is *marturouminos*. The same word appears in Acts 10:22 in reference to the Roman centurion, Cornelius. It was said of Cornelius that he was a man of good reputation among the Jews. The underlying meaning of *marturouminos* is "attestation to character."

◇ Why is it important to have a good reputation with unbelievers as well as believers?

_____

_____

◇ What is required of Life-giving leaders in order to build good reputations for themselves? Among those they lead?

_____

_____

2. Full of the Holy Spirit:

The design of the Holy Spirit, as He develops in us fruit that is characteristic of the Divine nature, is to constrain us toward a life in which the tendencies of the flesh are both undesirable and unproductive and to release us into a ministry in which every disciple of the Lord Jesus Christ fulfills the call to become "kings and priests" in Him (Rev. 1:6). Being filled with the Holy Spirit is not a one-time event. It is instead, an ongoing flow of the living God to His disciples who, in turn, minister His life, love, grace, peace, and wholeness to others.

◇ How would you compare the fruit of the Spirit (Gal. 5:22, 23) with the works of the flesh (vv. 19–21)?

_____

_____

◇ When a person walks in the Spirit, what will happen? (v. 16)

_____

_____

The word "walk" in verse 16 (Greek *peripateo*) means "to walk at large, especially as proof of ability"; "to be occupied with or engaged in." The tense of this verb implies progression or steady progress in grace. The Holy Spirit both monitors and empowers, enabling practical godliness.

Growth in Christ increases resistance to all that is uncharacteristic of Him. We become more internally motivated as our hearts learn to inhibit disobedience, instead of relying on our minds to memorize rules and wrestle to obey. Learning to "walk in the Spirit" will bring a gradual movement from mental rules and disciplines to obedience rooted in the heart's judgements and convictions.

◇ How does walking in the Spirit form God's character in you?

_____

◇ How does being full of the Holy Spirit attract people to Christ?

3. Full of Wisdom:

The sixth chapter of Acts says that Stephen, "full of faith and power, did great wonders and signs among the people" (v. 8). It also says that Stephen's enemies could not "resist the wisdom and the Spirit by which he spoke" (v. 10). Check out the full meaning of this kind of wisdom from the Word Wealth definition.

WORD WEALTH

Wisdom, *sophia* (Acts 6:10). Practical wisdom, prudence, skill, comprehensive insight, Christian enlightenment, a right application of knowledge, insight into the true nature of things. Wisdom in the Bible is often coupled with knowledge (Rom. 11:33; 1 Cor. 12:8; Col. 2:3). In anticipation of our needing guidance, direction, and knowing, God tells us to ask for wisdom, assuring us of a liberal reception (James 1:5).

◇ Write God's promise to you from James 1:5.

◇ Why is God-given wisdom such an important quality to have?

FAITH ALIVE

◇ How can a leader minister fullness of the Holy Spirit and wisdom to others?

◈ How can these qualities be developed in your own life as well?

PAUL'S LEADERSHIP GUIDELINES

Scripture says that a man who desires the position of "bishop" desires a good thing (1 Tim. 3:1). The office of "bishop" is not the monarchial episcopate, which developed later. The Greek word *episkopos* designates a local pastoral oversight. Hence, in our culture a word that clearly expresses the meaning of "bishop" is "supervisor" or "overseer."

The apostle Paul wrote two major passages that give a comprehensive profile for testing spiritual maturity or qualifications for leadership. Note that Paul's emphasis is more on "being" than on "doing." Here is a combined list from 1 Timothy 3:2–7 and Titus 1:6–9:

Blameless; the husband of one wife; temperate; sober-minded; of good behavior; hospitable; able to teach; not given to wine; not violent; not greedy for money; gentle; not quarrelsome; not covetous; one who rules his own house well with his children in submission; not a novice; has a good testimony among those who are outside; not self-willed; not quick-tempered; lover of what is good; responsible steward; just; holy; self-controlled; holds fast to the Word.

After reading this, you may feel that no one can fulfill such a high standard! Bear in mind that while we may not see each of these qualities in their completeness, we are assured that our character formation is in process and that the Holy Spirit is at work. We can trust in God's love and grace as He transforms us into Christ's image.

Let's choose one of these characteristics from this list: "gentleness." This word often conjures up spineless, "milque-toast" images that really don't depict the true definition of gentleness at all! Study the Word Wealth entry for "gentle" before answering the questions.

WORD WEALTH

Gentle, *epieikes* (1 Timothy 3:3). From *epi*, "unto," and *eikos*, "likely." The word suggests a character that is equitable, reasonable, forbearing, moderate, fair, and considerate. It is the opposite of harsh, abrasive, sarcastic, cruel, and contentious. The person with *epieikes* does not insist on the letter of the law.

◇ What is the biblical definition of gentleness?

◇ Does a gentle person insist that everything must be done per-fectly? How would a gentle person administer correction?

◇ Go back to the list of qualifications for leaders from Titus and 1 Timothy. Select at least three and write your thoughts about each. (What is this quality about? How can you imple-ment it into your process of growth?)

1.

2.

3.

KINGDOM EXTRA

With the aid of a study Bible, commentary, Greek lexicon, or other resource materials, discover the expanded meanings of the words and phrases used in 1 Timothy 3:2–6. The following ques-tions will assist you in your discovery.

◇ v. 2: Does the word "blameless" imply perfection? If not, what does it mean?

◈ v. 2: What does "the husband of one wife" imply? Does this mean the spiritual leader cannot be single? Not divorced? Not widowed? Not remarried? Not a polygamist?

_____

_____

◈ vv. 2, 3: List the positive and negative traits found in these verses.

Positive _____

_____

_____

Negative _____

_____

_____

◈ vv. 4, 5: Why is it so important for the spiritual leader to have success in managing the home?

_____

_____

◈ v. 6: What are the dangers inherent in appointing a new convert as an overseer of the church?

_____

_____

The 1 Timothy passage continues with the subject of leadership by dealing with the qualifications for deacons and their wives. The New Testament does not define the exact nature and duties of the office of deacon, but the meaning of the word suggests the function as an attendant.

◈ What qualities should a deacon have? (1 Tim. 3:8–12)

_____

_____

A study of leader qualifications is not complete without stressing faithfulness to the Word of God. In Titus, Paul speaks of sound doctrine (1:9), sound faith (1:13) and sound speech (2:8). The teaching, belief, and testimony of those called to Christian leadership needs to be grounded in the Word of the gospel.

◇ How does a good leader "hold fast the faithful word"?

_____

_____

FAITH ALIVE

◇ Of these qualities that are desirable for Life-giving leadership, which ones do you feel are strengths in your life?

_____

_____

◇ List those characteristics that need development or improvement in your life. How can you partner with God or an accountability prayer partner to see growth in these areas?

_____

_____

A LONG WAY TO GO?

It is likely that once people understand the standards for leadership, they will see areas in which they fall short. Rather than disqualifying us for ministry, we can be brought to growth. One way this happens is through our willingness to be accountable and teachable in relationship with trustworthy persons.

◇ Turn to Ephesians 5:21. What does it say to do?

_____

_____

Submission is taking our divinely ordered place in a relationship. Submission can never be required by one human being of another; it can only be given on the basis of trust, that is, by believing in God's Word and being willing to learn to grow in relationships.

◇ What does Scripture say will happen when we confess our trespasses and pray with one another? (James 5:16)

_____

_____

Also, essential to the growth of leaders is our willingness to renew our minds through the Word and to sustain the fullness of the Holy Spirit in our lives.

◇ In seeking to maintain personal integrity, what is your response to the following three passages?

Romans 12:1, 2 _____

_____

2 Corinthians 10:4, 5 _____

_____

Ephesians 5:17–20 _____

_____

Remember that while true godliness is conduct consistent with the character of Christ, character growth is a process. The Father's goal for our lives is to grow us up to be like His Son—to conform us to Christ's image (Rom. 8:29). As our lives progressively demonstrate the truth and love of God in Jesus Christ, people will be drawn to faith as they see what He is really like.

FAITH ALIVE

◇ How does a Life-giving leader implement leadership standards for others who wish to serve without discouraging others' process of growth in character?

_____

_____

◇ How does a good spiritual leader encourage character growth in others?

_____

_____

OPENNESS
Lesson 5

THE BIG IDEA

The key to powerful impact in ministry is honesty. Being open and approachable makes one a better and more trusted leader.

A leader who is honest is transparent with God, others and themselves, thereby modeling Christ's openness and Spirit-motivated life. To be open means to be vulnerable, having the ability to humbly share one's own struggles and victories, and to be empathetic toward others.

VULNERABILITY—VALUE VS. COST

Jesus did not have to be vulnerable; He *chose* to be vulnerable. The very fact that He was willing to be arrested and humbled on the Cross demonstrates this. During His arrest, He demonstrated His willingness to be vulnerable, despite the cost.

◇ In an attempt to defend Jesus, Peter cut off the ear of one of those who came to arrest Him (Luke 22:50; John 18:10). How did Jesus respond to the man's injury? (Luke 22:51)

_____

_____

_____

Consider this point: when Jesus reached out to heal the ear of His enemy, He made Himself vulnerable to a return sword thrust. (His reaching for the man's head easily could have been interpreted as another hostile move.) The lesson here is that vulnerability may expose us to misunderstanding, but it also will bring healing.

Being vulnerable as a leader means to stand totally open as a human being, hiding nothing and refusing to defend oneself. Few things elicit more of a response from people than the sense that they are dealing with someone who feels their pain and understands their need. This discovery is possible only if the leader is vulnerable enough to disclose his or her own pain and needs.

◇ How is it possible that Jesus can sympathize with our weaknesses? (Heb. 4:14)

_____

_____

FAITH ALIVE

◇ Have you ever reached out to a hurting person, and that person struck you back? What is the biblical and best way to respond?

_____

_____

◇ What is the value of a Life-giving leader's being vulnerable when ministering to others? What is the potential cost? How does Jesus' example encourage you?

_____

_____

_____

JESUS IS APPROACHABLE

The Gospels are full of accounts that reveal the openness and approachableness of Christ. People with insurmountable problems and physical needs followed Him wherever He went. He took the time to listen to their needs and respond to them compassionately. So secure was He in His own personal identity and mission that He could make Himself available to the people. Instead of distancing Himself, He invited them to come to Him with all their problems.

◇ What did Jesus say to those who "labor and are heavy laden"? (Matt. 11:28, 29)

_____

_____

45

See what you can glean from each of these four situations that reveal Jesus' accessibility.

1. Feeding the Four Thousand (Matt. 15:32–39)

◇ Prior to this miracle, how many days had Jesus spent with the multitude? How do you think He felt physically after that length of time?

_____

_____

◇ What did the disciples learn about leadership as a result of this miracle?

_____

_____

◇ How can you apply the lessons the disciples learned to your own call to serve others?

_____

_____

2. Two Blind Men (Matt. 20:29–34)

◇ Jesus had important business to tend to. But on His way to Jerusalem to be honored (Matt. 21:9) and then crucified (Matt. 27:35), He encountered two blind men who cried out for ministry. The crowd warned the blind men to be quiet. What did Jesus do? (20:32–34)

_____

_____

◇ Have you ever become impatient with someone who pressed you to pray for them or minister to their need at an inconvenient time?

_____

_____

◇ What can you learn from the persistence of the two blind men? What can you learn from Jesus' response?

_____

3. Jesus Blessing the Children (Mark 10:13–16)

◇ Why do you suppose the disciples wanted to keep the children away from Jesus?

_____

_____

◇ Apparently the disciples felt that children were too insignificant to be allowed to interrupt the work of Jesus. How did Jesus feel about them?

_____

_____

◇ In what ways can spiritual leaders demonstrate their love and concern for children?

_____

_____

4. The Woman of Samaria (John 4:3–30)

Here, Jesus is reaching out to a woman who was of a different ethnicity and whose morals were questionable. This is consistent with Jesus' frequent "reachings": Breaking the mold of the traditionally "religious," He became a "friend" of tax collectors and the generally sinful who were not only loathed by the supposedly "righteous," but were thought to be unworthy of attention (Luke 5:27–31). Jesus gave time and energy to relationships, which sometimes meant experiencing pain and loss (John 11:35, 38).

◇ How did Jesus handle awkward encounters with people?

_____

_____

◇ What is Jesus teaching us about our accessibility to people who are considered social or religious outcasts in society?

_____

_____

_____

_____

PAUL SHARES OPENLY

It was important to the apostle Paul that people saw him as a growing, Spirit-motivated leader. He wasn't hesitant to share his weakness, fears, and faults at times.

Ordinarily Paul did not "boast" about his apostolic gifts, the successes of his ministry, or the incredible sufferings he endured in his service to Christ. But in his second letter to the Corinthians, he found it necessary to become "boastful" to the point of appearing foolish by revealing details about the sufferings he endured as an apostle. Paul wrote about his vulnerabilities so that the believers at Corinth might be pointed to God as they compared Paul's true calling and experiences with those of false apostles.

To discover the degree of vulnerability that Paul disclosed to the church at Corinth, turn to the verses from 2 Corinthians listed below. Then record the vulnerability or struggle of this great leader in the right column.

2 Corinthians	Paul's Vulnerability/Struggle
11:1–4	
11:5–15	
11:16–21	
11:22–33	
12:1–6	
12:7–10	
12:11–13	

✧ God told Paul that His strength is made perfect in what condition? (2 Cor. 12:9)

_____

_____

✧ In the midst of conflict at Macedonia, how did Paul feel inside? (2 Cor. 7:5)

_____

_____

✧ How did God respond to Paul's fear and weariness? (v. 6)

_____

_____

✧ Paul describes himself in 1 Corinthians 2:3–5 as a person with weakness and fear at times. How is God glorified in that? (v. 5)

_____

_____

FAITH ALIVE

✧ Do you think Paul's willingness to share with others encouraged them to trust God in their own distresses? Why or why not?

_____

_____

✧ How can a leader be honest without losing credibility?

_____

_____

FREEDOM IN ACCOUNTABILITY

Paul did not hide his weaknesses; rather, he saw them as strengths because God's power was glorified in his weaknesses. Let's study now the value of accountability and transparency of character.

◈ Solomon saw the worth of wise counsel. What did he say about having many counselors? (Prov. 15:22)

_____

_____

Openness to wise counsel will lead to accountability to ourselves, to others, and to God. Accountability can be defined as a willingness to be responsible for our thoughts, words, and deeds. It comes from the financial term "account" which demonstrates negative _debits_ as well as positive _credits_. The Word Wealth gives more insight into this important word. In this context, Abraham's belief in God was "accounted to him for righteousness."

WORD WEALTH

Accounted, _logidzomai_ (Rom. 4:3). Compare "logistic" and "logarithm." Numerically, to count, compute, calculate, sum up. Metaphorically, to consider, reckon, reason, deem, evaluate, value. _Logidzomai_ finalizes thought, judges matters, draws logical conclusions, decides outcomes, and puts every action into a debit or credit position.

When we choose to be accountable, we accept responsibility for our thoughts, words, and actions before God, within ourselves and with others. This goes against the grain of our society—as well as our natural tendencies—but holds great reward in the kingdom of God. For Life-giving leaders, transparent accountability is essential to the health of their ministry. Briefly, let's examine why.

1. Accountability toward God: Our relationship with God is based on the truth of His accountability towards us. God accounts for our sins through the death, burial, and Resurrection of Jesus Christ. God takes into account that we need a Savior and has provided one. In addition, our ongoing relationship with God is defined by our willingness to be accountable to Him regarding the areas we need to address—both good and bad. God wants us to account for the blessings as well as the sin in our lives.

◈ What level of transparency before God does David describe in Psalm 139:23, 24?

_____

_____

◇ How are we to draw near to God? (Heb. 10:21, 22)

◇ To whom are we to be reconciled? What is our message as Christ's ambassadors? (2 Cor. 5:19–21)

---

2. Personal accountability: This is the ability to be honest with ourselves regarding our shortcomings as well as our successes. Accountability is the opposite of denial. Without honest accountability to oneself, a person closes the door on Spirit-Filled living and resigns oneself to a life of mediocrity, unreal expectations and disillusionment, defeat, frustration, and anxiety.

◇ David wrote Psalm 51 after the prophet Nathan had confronted him about his adulterous affair and cover-up. Read this Psalm in its entirety.

◇ How do we know that David had broken through denial of his sin and repented? (vv. 3, 4)

◇ What did David pray in order to be restored? (vv. 7–12)

◇ Could David have been restored if he hadn't honestly acknowledged his sin?

◇ God desires truth to go deep inside to our "inward . . . hidden part." What will God reveal to us there? (v. 6)

◈ Now, turn to the New Testament. How does denying and hiding sin block spiritual progress? (1 John 1:6–10)

_____

_____

◈ How does honest confession bring freedom? (v. 9)

_____

_____

◈ If we walk in the light, what will be the result? Who else is in the light with us? (v. 7)

_____

_____

_____

◈ Will we experience His cleansing if we shield our failure from Him? Why or why not?

_____

_____

_____

_____

Scripture says we are to make an honest evaluation of ourselves: We are not to think of ourselves more highly than we ought to think; instead, we need to think soberly (Rom. 12:3). The word "soberly" in this context means to be of sound mind, to be self-controlled, moderate, and able to reason. It is taken from the Greek *sozo*, which means "to save", and *phren*, meaning "the mind." The implication is that through honest faith, we will be realistic in our assessment of our place in God's plan.

3. Accountability toward others: Most of us in North America are taught to be independent and self-reliant. To be accountable to others seems to go against our preconceived ideas of what a Christian leader is to be. However, the exact opposite is true. Practicing healthy biblical accountability toward our brothers and sisters in Christ is appropriate and necessary to overcome our sin and become mature in our relationship with the Lord. Accountability is an integral part of healing and restoration in Christ.

◇ Solomon uses an image to describe how true friendship works. What is that image? (Prov. 27:17)

◇ How did David describe the weight of his sin? (Ps. 38:4)

◇ How important is confession of sin and praying for one another? (James 5:14–16)

◇ When we are accountable to one another, what happens? (James 5:16)

You may think, *this is all well and good, but how do I go about implementing principles of accountability in my ministry as well as in my personal life?* You can start by being a team player with your ministry team. Schedule meetings, retreats, and training sessions for the purpose of providing opportunities for the leadership team to receive wise counsel and to be accountable to one another. Encourage your leadership team to find personal accountability partners (always same-gender partners). Also, it is important for you to develop or deepen relationship with an accountability partner yourself. Don't have one? Try looking to other leaders in the city, or to your supervisor or a mature, trusted friend for this support.

However God leads you (or your leadership team) to greater accountability, know that God-inspired accountability always leads men and women to a place of strength in the Lord. As people are honest and reveal their vulnerabilities as well as their assets, they are built up, not torn down. It is in the beauty of the Lord's way that people find freedom, strength, healing, and support as they confess their sins in transparent and trusting relationships.

FAITH ALIVE

Take a moment to ponder the two big hindrances to transparent, accountable relationships—fear and isolation.

1. Fear says: *Will the person reject me? Will I be accepted, warts and all? Will others I lead become discouraged if they find out I'm struggling?*

◇ List other fears that could keep you (or those you lead) from being accountable to themselves, to others, or to God.

_____

_____

_____

◇ In order to conquer that fear, list the benefits of healthy accountability. Use some of the scriptures you studied to help form your list.

_____

_____

2. Isolation works to keep you disconnected from healthy, accountable relationships with others.

◇ Think about the kinds of situations that tend to isolate you (or those you lead).

_____

_____

◇ List current relationships that have the potential of developing into accountable relationships.

_____

_____

◇ How can a good leader encourage others to find and develop accountability prayer partners?

_____

_____

In this chapter, we have studied the importance of being open and available to people, seeing Jesus as our example. Our perceived vulnerabilities and weaknesses do not have to disqualify or isolate us; rather they can become our strengths as we learn to submit them to the Lord and allow the Holy Spirit greater reign in our ministry and our lives. As part of that process, the Life-giving leaders will find freedom as we leaders model accountability in every aspect of our lives and teach that to others.

Surrender Control, Release Gifting

Lesson 6

The Big Idea

God's way of leading—His leadership style, if you will—is unique in our culture, for He does not seek to control or to impress. Discover the joy of releasing His purpose through the gifts He has bestowed upon each believer—and specifically, on you.

Which Leadership Style Is Best?

Opinions vary on how to implement leadership in the church. The purpose of this chapter is not to say one leadership "model" is right and another wrong. Rather, the focus is on biblical truth to guide you as God leads you in your call to serve others.

One thing is clear: human magnetism, influence, or genius does not power biblical leadership. Personal charm may garner a leader a following for a while, but charm alone will wear thin quickly if not accompanied by substantive ministry that feeds the spirit and gives biblical direction for life. People of discernment hunger for Jesus and need leaders who can lead them both to Him and in a deeper walk with Him in Spirit and in truth (God's Word).

◇ Who do the lost need to see? (John 12:21)

_____

_____

_____

◇ What was the foundation of John the Baptist's ministry? (John 3:27)

_____

_____

_____

◈ John says in verse 3:30, "He [God] must increase, but I must decrease." Does that mean a leader's effectiveness or presence diminishes as He points people to Jesus? What does it mean?

_____

_____

God alone is the only sure foundation. It is important that spiritual leaders point people to the Rock, upon which they may securely build their lives, instead of pointing people to rely on human endeavors.

FAITH ALIVE

◈ *God must increase, but I must decrease.* List practical ways you can implement this truth as you grow toward becoming a Life-giving leader.

_____

_____

◈ How does a good leader serve others so as to direct their attention and their loyalties to Christ alone and not to human leadership?

_____

_____

LEADERSHIP IS NOT CONTROL

The people of Jesus' day were familiar with two kinds of leadership, both of which exercised negative control over the people. These were demonstrated: (1) through the hierarchical system of rulership that Gentile leaders used and (2) by the way the Jewish religious leaders exercised control over the people through legalism and false guilt. It is important to delve into these systems because they are just as prevalent today. Much can be gleaned about what *not* to do from these negative examples.

◈ What did Jesus say about the Gentile leaders? (Matt. 20:25)

_____

_____

◇ How does Jesus define leadership? (Matt. 20:26–28)

_____

The Jewish religious leaders of Christ's time were supposed to be models for the people to follow. However, they were quite the opposite, for they perceived themselves as apart from and above others. Jesus made it quite clear that these leaders had a religious outward form but were devoid of inner spiritual reality. Their words and actions did not match their hearts' condition.

◇ What graphic term did Jesus use to describe the hypocrisy of the scribes and Pharisees? (Matt. 23:27)

_____

◇ How did these religious leaders appear outwardly? What was the truth about their inward condition? (23:28)

_____

_____

◇ How did Jesus want them to lead? (23:11, 12)

_____

_____

◇ Jesus healed a woman of a rigidly fused spine on the Sabbath (Luke 13:10–13). The religious ruler of the synagogue was furious because he thought Jesus had broken a religious law. How did Jesus respond? (vv. 15, 16)

_____

_____

A servant does not seek to control, but seeks opportunities to serve others. Jesus perfectly modeled this servant spirit. Rather than controlling people, He set them free.

FAITH ALIVE

◇ How do you think the religious leaders of Jesus' time thought about themselves?

_____

◇ How does an attitude of self-righteousness blind a person from the true purpose of ministry?

_____

_____

◇ What is the true gauge of success in leadership?

_____

_____

LEADERSHIP INVOLVES OTHERS

A wise leader recognizes the value of teamwork. Our model is Jesus, who chose, taught, and released ministry through His disciples. The apostle Paul also realized that the mission of the church is effective when the leadership team works together.

◇ What should be the goal of any leadership team? (Phil. 1:27)

_____

_____

◇ How does Paul characterize the relationship between God and workers in the church? (1 Cor. 3:9)

_____

_____

◇ What image does Paul use to describe the relationships within the church? How does this apply to a leadership team? (Col. 2:2)

_____

_____

LEADERSHIP RELEASES GIFTS

A wise leader will also recognize the value of the giftings and ministries that God has placed in the church. These gifts are given for the nurture and equipping of His church, not for hierarchical control or ecclesiastical competition.

How does the Bible define a spiritual gift, and how does it work? The apostle Paul told the Corinthian church he was grateful that they came "short in no gift." (1 Cor. 1:7). Let's examine the Word

Wealth meaning for the word "gift," which is rooted in the Greek word *charisma.*

WORD WEALTH

Gift, *charisma* (1 Cor. 1:7). This word is related to other words derived from the root *char*. *Chara* is joy, cheerfulness, delight. *Charis* is grace, goodwill, undeserved favor. *Charisma* is a gift of grace, a free gift, divine gratuity, spiritual endowment, miraculous faculty. It is especially used to designate the gifts of the Spirit (1 Cor. 12:4–10). In modern usage, a "charismatic" signifies one who either has one or more of these gifts functioning in his life, or who believes these gifts are for today's church.

◇ God's gift and God's grace share what common root word? What is the significance of that?

_____

_____

_____

_____

The abundance of gifts to the church reflects the love and care that God has for each of us. It is His will that each believer enjoy the fullness of the Spirit, grow to full stature in Christ, and be equipped to minister.

TYPES OF GIFTS

All gifts spring from God's grace. Some gifts deal with basic life purpose and motivation, some gifts equip and facilitate the church body and gifts, and the *charismata* gifts are given by the Holy Spirit. You will study briefly three places in Scripture where the gifts are explained and their purpose given.

1. The *charismata* gifts, given by the Holy Spirit (1 Cor. 12:7–10)

Paul defines a spiritual gift in this context as a supernatural ability bestowed on an individual by the Holy Spirit, not as a heightened natural ability. Thus, each gift is a manifestation of the Spirit, that is, visible evidence of His activity. The Holy Spirit bestows the gifts to whom He wills as the occasion recommends from the divine viewpoint.

◈ Turn to 1 Corinthians 12:7. To whom is the manifestation of the Holy Spirit given? Who gains from this?

These gifts specify the varied distribution necessary for a full manifestation of the Spirit:

The word of wisdom is a spiritual utterance at a given moment through the Spirit, supernaturally disclosing the mind, purpose, and will of God as applied to a specific situation.

The word of knowledge is a supernatural revelation of information pertaining to a person or an event, given for a specific purpose, usually having to do with an immediate need.

The gift of faith is a unique form of faith that goes beyond natural faith and saving faith. It supernaturally trusts and does not doubt with reference to the specific matters involved.

Gifts of healings are those healings that God performs supernaturally by the Spirit. The plural suggests that as there are many sicknesses and diseases, the gift is related to healings of many disorders.

The working of miracles is a manifestation of power beyond the ordinary course of natural law. It is a divine enablement to do something that could not be done naturally.

Prophecy is a divine disclosure on behalf of the Spirit, an edifying Revelation of the Spirit for the moment (1 Cor. 14:3), a sudden insight of the Spirit, prompting exhortation or comfort (14:3, 30).

Discerning of spirits is the ability to discern the spirit world, and especially to detect the true source of circumstances or motives of people.

Different kind of tongues is the gift of speaking supernaturally in a language not known to the individual. The plural allows different forms, possibly harmonizing the known spoken languages of Acts 2:4–6 and the unknown transrational utterances in Corinthians, designed particularly for praying and singing in the Spirit, mostly for private worship (1 Cor. 14:14–19).

The interpretation of tongues is the gift of rendering the transrational (but not irrational) message of the Spirit meaningful to others when exercised in public. It is not the translation of a foreign language.

Note: none of the gifts require a public setting, although each may and should be welcomed in corporate gatherings.

◇ Reread the definitions. In what way do these nine spiritual gifts encourage and strengthen people in the body of Christ?

_____

_____

2. Basic life purpose and motivation gifts (Rom. 12:6–8)

Being aware of spiritual gifts creates confidence in spiritual leaders. Knowing that God appoints and enables, let us take the necessary steps to discover what gifts we possess.

◇ Match the name of the gift listed in Romans 12:6–8 with its description.

_____ Refers to: (1) those in the public office of teacher; (2) those who are specially gifted to keep an eye on and instruct the revealed truth of God's Word, regardless of public office.

_____ Defines: (1) those with the special gift of strong, perceptive emotions; (2) those called to special functions of Christian relief or acts of charity.

_____ Refers to: (1) those whose creation gift from the Father enables them to view all of life with special ongoing prophetic insight, independent of public office or special use by the Spirit in giving public prophecy; (2) the manifestation of public prophecy, speaking something that God has spontaneously brought to mind.

_____ Refers to: (1) those who are gifted to effectively facilitate all areas of life; (2) those with the public function of administration (or possibly even to a deacon).

_____ Suggests: (1) those whose special creation gift enables them to most effectively serve the body in physical ways; (2) the rendering of any type of service by anyone in the church.

_____ Describes: (1) those whose creation gift enables them to best apply God's truth through encouragement; (2) those (such as pastors) who are called to publicly bring encouragement to the church.

_____ Refers to: (1) those gifted to contribute to the emotional and/or physical support of others; (2) those gifted with abundant financial means so as to support the work of the gospel.

KINGDOM EXTRA

There are basically two interpretative approaches to the Romans 12:6–8 passage on gifts: (1) To see them as a category distinct from that of other New Testament passages, often referred to as the Father's creational gifts; or (2) to see them as a repeat or overlap of many of those mentioned in either 1 Corinthians 12:12–29 or Ephesians 4:11.

FAITH ALIVE

◇   What are the spiritual gifts that function in your ministry?

_____

_____

◇   How did you become aware of those gifts being present in your life and ministry?

_____

_____

3. Gifts to equip and facilitate the church body (Eph. 4:11, 12)

These gifts equip (mend, prepare, and enable for function) each member of the body of Christ.

◇   Turn to Ephesians 4. List the gifts given in verse 11.

_____

_____

_____

KINGDOM EXTRA

Some have debated the place of apostles in the modern-day church. Beyond the distinct role filled by the original founding apostles (Eph. 2:20; Rev. 21:14), the New Testament mentions enough additional apostles to indicate that this office, with that of prophets, is as continuing a ministry in the church as the more commonly acknowledged offices of evangelists, pastors, and teachers (some make pastor-teacher one office).

◈ What are the two purposes for the gifts according to Ephesians 4:12?

_____

_____

It is interesting to note that the Greek word for *equipping* implies: (1) a recovered wholeness as when a broken limb is set and mends; (2) a discovered function, as when a physical member is properly operating. The *work of ministry* is the enterprise of each member of the body of Christ and not the exclusive charge of select leaders. The task of the gifted leader is to cultivate the individual and corporate ministries of those he or she leads.

◈ What is the ultimate goal of the spiritual gifts? (vv. 13–16)

_____

_____

◈ How can a leader cultivate these kinds of gifts?

_____

_____

Paul encouraged his son in the faith, Timothy, to make the fullest use of the spiritual equipment given to him for ministry. Paul wrote, "Stir up the gift of God which is in you through the laying on of my hands" (2 Tim. 1:6). It is interesting that this word "gift" is the same Greek word, *charisma*, that we studied earlier from 1 Corinthians 1:7. This suggests a distinct manifestation of the Holy Spirit bestowed upon Timothy through the prayers of the apostle and others.

FAITH ALIVE

What do you think it means to "stir up the gift of God"? How can you apply this to your experience?

EVERYBODY CONTRIBUTES AND BENEFITS

True supernatural ministry at work in the church begets vital, spiritually functional people throughout the whole church family. The body is to be built up by the mutual efforts of all the members supplying their contribution to the whole. The call to empower people requires mentoring, training, imparting, and discipling—all aimed at preparing the body to become an overflow of the ministering life of Jesus Christ to others, in their city, their nation, and their world.

FAITH ALIVE

◇ What criteria does the Bible set forth to place people in their ministry roles?

_____

_____

_____

◇ What are some ways a Life-giving leader can encourage others to find and use their gifts?

_____

_____

_____

_____

PRAYER

Lesson 7

THE BIG IDEA

The invitation of God's kingdom authority into our circumstances and our world brings forth the power of heaven's rule to change, transform, and deliver. Prayer is the match that lights the fuse, releasing the explosive power of the Holy Spirit. Come experience the kind of intercession that makes a difference in our world.

A Sunday school teacher was concerned because his high school students did not know Christ as Savior. In spite of his thorough lesson preparations and fun activities, their interest in spiritual things seemed to lag. The teacher tried everything. But it was not until he spent time in fasting and prayer, praying earnestly for each student by name, that a change came. The teenagers' interest in spiritual things increased, and there were fewer distractions in the class. Over a period of a few weeks, the teacher saw the rewards of his intercession as each student accepted Christ as Savior.

JESUS, OUR EXAMPLE IN PRAYER

"Now in the morning, having risen a long while before daylight, He went out and departed to a solitary place; and there He prayed" (Mark 1:35). That says it all! Jesus, the Son of God who had commanded the seas to be still, who had demonstrated power over demons and disease, who raised the dead, showed the need of prayer for sustained spiritual effectiveness.

We see Jesus going to His heavenly Father often, and at critical points of His life. With regard to each of these verses, what did Jesus pray? Why? What can we learn from that?

1. Before extended ministry (Mark 1:35–39)

2. Before choosing the twelve apostles (Luke 6:12, 13)

3. Before the Cross (Luke 22:39–46)

4. On the Cross (Luke 23:34)

Jesus depended upon prayer to His heavenly Father in order to receive strength, wisdom, discernment, and direction. It was in prayer that Jesus found the grace and courage to make the ultimate sacrifice, the giving of His life so that others might have eternal life. But Jesus' prayers did not stop at the Cross; they continue to this day.

◇ Jesus always lives to do what ministry? (Heb. 7:25)

_____

_____

◇ Who are the ones who receive the benefit of Jesus' intercession? (Rom. 8:34)

_____

_____

◇ It is a blessing to know that Jesus is in heaven praying for us. How do we know that He sympathizes with our weaknesses? (Heb. 4:15)

_____

_____

FAITH ALIVE

Jesus prayed before every major ministry decision or event—sometimes He prayed all night. What does that tell us of the importance of communing with our heavenly Father? The Life-giving leader determines to pray not only whenever we face difficult times or tough ministry decisions but also to seek God daily for guidance and grace regarding every detail of our life.

How does Jesus' example of prayer give you confidence that no matter what you face, you can be strengthened through prayer?

WHY PRAY?

One of Jesus' disciples asked Him to teach them to pray (Luke 11:1). In response to that request, Jesus said a prayer that has come to be known as "The Lord's Prayer." This prayer serves as our model for daily communication with our heavenly Father.

◇ Read the Lord's Prayer in Luke 11:2–4, noting the different parts to it.

_____

_____

_____

_____

◇ How are we to pray with respect to God's kingdom? (v. 10)

_____

_____

_____

Jesus' words "Your kingdom come" are more than a suggestion to pray for a distant millennial day, for everything in this prayer is current. This prayer is not a formula for repetition so much as it is an outline for expansion. Worship is to be longer than a sentence. Petitions are not confined to bread alone. Forgiveness is to be requested in specifics, not generalities, and prayer for the entry of God's kingdom into present earthborn situations is not accomplished in a momentary utterance. The verb mood and tense of "Your kingdom come" essentially says, "Father, let Your kingdom come here and now!"

Such prayerful intervention is called *intercession.* Motivation toward such prayer occurs when we recognize the importance Jesus placed on prayer as helping us serve in our roles as "kingdom administrators."

Without the intervention of God's kingdom rule through prayer, earth's circumstances will succumb to inevitable consequences. Earthly scenes of need must be penetrated by God's will here "as in heaven" or either the weakness of man's rule (the flesh) or the viciousness of hell's works (the devil) will prevail in its stead. God's power alone can change things and bring heaven's rule (kingdom) to earth. The honor and the glory for answers to prayer belong to Him.

However, the praying is ours to do: unless we ask for the intervention of His kingdom and obey His prayer-lessons, nothing will change. The power is His, but the privilege to ask in prayer is ours.

All kingdom ministry begins with, is sustained by, and will triumph through prayer.

FAITH ALIVE

What situations in your life need an intervention of God's kingdom rule? Using the Lord's Prayer as a pattern, incorporate into your prayer life these needs, asking God's kingdom to reign there.

STAND IN THE GAP

The heart of God is searching for those who will "stand in the gap" in prayer on behalf of people who are being diminished or destroyed. We see a vivid picture of this in the Book of Ezekiel where people were being robbed, violated, oppressed, mistreated, and murdered. (Sounds like much of our world today, doesn't it?)

◇ Read Ezekiel 22:25–29. What were some of the horrendous things that were taking place?

_____

_____

_____

◇ God was looking for a person to stop the tide of destruction. What did He want this person to do? (v. 30)

_____

_____

_____

A study of the Word Wealth entry illuminates understanding of what it means to "stand in the gap."

Gap, *perets* (Ezek. 22:30). A break, gap, or breach; especially a gap in a wall. *Perets* comes from the verb *parats*, "to break forth, break open, or break down." *Perets* occurs about 25 times. Two verses (Is. 58:12; Amos 9:11) show that gaps or breaches need to be repaired; the former verse refers to the physical and spiritual ruins of Zion, and the latter to the tabernacle of David. In Ezekiel

22:30, standing in the gap is a metaphor for committed intercession. There is a gap between God and man that an intercessor tries
to repair.

The picture is clear. Without someone interceding in prayer,
invasion by the darkness occurs, and eventual destruction of people takes place. But the Old Testament gives hope of the availabil-
ity of an Intercessor, the coming Messiah, whose intercessory work
is eternal (Is. 59:16; 63:5. See also Heb. 7:24, 25).

There are examples throughout the Old and New Testaments
where standing in the gap through prayer turned the tide for a situation. Let's read three cases where intercession made a difference. For each verse, write what situation was reversed through
intercession.

◈   Deuteronomy 9:25–29; 10:10, 11 _____

_____

_____

◈   Acts 4:29–31 _____

_____

_____

◈   Acts 12:5–12 _____

_____

Never underestimate the possibility of any reversal of a situation through the prayers of a loving intercessor. As you pray for
the seemingly impossible, aim to never limit God's ability or min-
imize the effectiveness of your partnership with Him in prayer. Be
encouraged that although you may need to stand in prayer for
many years to witness God's answer, or it may even occur beyond
your lifetime, God's promises to us are faithful and His answers
are sure.

YOUR PRAYER MAP

What do we do when we don't know how to get to a destination?
We consult a map to find our way. Similarly, God provides in His
Word direction on how His people are to seek Him through prayer
to see restoration and revival.

◈ List three basic things that God's people are to do in intercession to see breakthrough. (2 Chr. 7:14)

1. _____

2. _____

3. _____

◈ What will God do in response to intercessory prayer? (2 Chr. 7:14)

1. _____

2. _____

3. _____

FAITH ALIVE

Focus on one of the three principles of intercessory prayer from these verses. What does it mean? How does a Life-giving leader implement it? Make it a goal to include this focus in your prayer time with the Lord this week.

THE SPIRIT'S DIRECTION

It is important for us to realize that we can't truly intercede effectively on the sole basis of our understanding. The fact that there are no "set formulas" in prayer is what makes prayer so exciting. Since we never really thoroughly know how to pray, we need to exercise humility and faith to wait on God and let the Holy Spirit direct us.

◈ How does the Holy Spirit help us pray when we don't know *what* to pray? (Rom. 8:26, 27)

_____

_____

_____

What an adventure it is to receive His insight and enablement for intercessory prayer. How can we know whether God wants to move through us with weeping, travailing, wrestling, fasting, the gifts of the Holy Spirit, dreams, visions, mental pictures, impressions, verses of Scripture quickened to us, or silence? By waiting on God and giving Him time, He will move on and through us.

◇ As we wait for God, what becomes our hope (expectation)? (Ps. 62:5)

_____

_____

HELPING PEOPLE TAKE PRAYER SERIOUSLY

It is one thing to believe in prayer and pray yourself; it is another thing to ignite others to want to pray. Much can be learned by the way God used Joel and Samuel to bring people to their knees in prayer.

SAMUEL

Samuel stepped forward to provide spiritual leadership to people lamenting their condition and not sure where to turn. His action demonstrates how confident leadership in corporate prayer can reopen the way for the fullness of God's work to be restored.

Turn to 1 Samuel 7:3–14. Read the five principles of leadership that Samuel used to bring the people back to God. After each action write the verse that describes it.

1. *The leader takes charge,* prophetically and with tender compassion—calling the people to renounce their sin, return to God, recommit themselves fully to Him, and seek His face together. (1 Sam. 7:3–____)
2. *The leader initiates prayer,* modeling it for others to follow—leading in fasting and in "pouring out" their hearts (as with the ceremonial water), dramatizing their heartfelt quest for God. (1 Sam. 7:____)
3. *The leader remains unceasing* in his prayers and in mobilizing the people for (spiritual) warfare. (1 Sam. 7:8–____)
4. *The leader helps people record* the manifest results of God's grace in answered prayer. (1 Sam. 7:____)
5. *The result is peace in the land.* (1 Sam. 7:____)

JOEL

When Joel was called to prophesy, the people were in sore defeat, famine, and despair, with no vision at all—not even for prayer. His sounding of the trumpet call to a sacred assembly opens to a prayer mobilization (Joel 2:1, 2). He does this by:

1. *Reviewing* the condition and helping the people conclude that they had no other recourse but to pray; and apart from divine intervention, they were finished. (Joel 2:3–____)
2. *Showing* the people the pathway to prayer with fasting and humility. (Joel 2:12–____)
3. *Declaring* God's promise if they would pray. (Joel 2:____–27)
4. *Prophetically declaring* an era of the Spirit's outpouring (Joel 2:28–____). This great passage leads us to Acts 2, the birthing of the church and the empowering of the Holy Spirit to form a spiritually empowered, praying, and ministering people. His enablement will help us assist others to pray with the same promise today, whatever the desperation of the circumstance.

KINGDOM EXTRA

In Isaiah 55:9, God reminds us that His ways and thoughts are unfathomably beyond ours. When you or those you lead intercede for the lost or for seemingly impossible situations, remember these truths:

1. Light is more powerful than darkness.
2. Truth is stronger than error.
3. There is more grace in God's heart than in people's hearts.
4. There is more power in the Holy Spirit to convict people of sin than there is power of satanic forces to tempt people to sin.
5. There is more power in one drop of the shed blood of the Lord Jesus to cleanse people's hearts from the stain of sin than there is in the accumulated filth of people's sin since Adam and Eve.

Now, using your concordance, Bible dictionary or other resource, find at least one Scripture reference that demonstrates each of those five principles of intercessory prayer.

FAITH ALIVE

As you grow in becoming a Life-giving leader, let yourself be stretched to a new level of intercession. In your times of intercession, pray that God will prepare you and other spiritual leaders for an awesome visitation of the Holy Spirit. For each day of the week, pray that believers you serve will:

Sunday: Have an understanding of the ways of the Spirit and will make room for God.

Monday: Be sensitive and flexible to flow with whatever new thing God wants to do.

Tuesday: Be taken over by the fear of the Lord and released from the fear of what people will think.

Wednesday: Recognize that the fear of the Lord is the source of their much-needed wisdom.

Thursday: Be given a deep desire to be radically real and to repent of all hypocrisy.

Friday: Be effective for the gospel in their assigned communities or missions around the world.

Saturday: Pray for the lost.

My own intercessory list: _____

_____

_____

_____

_____

_____

_____

_____

_____

REVIVAL
Lesson 8

THE BIG IDEA

God longs to see multitudes of people brought to salvation and changed by His power. What can a Life-giving leader do to prepare for this kind of revival? How do revival fires spread into and through the lives of a congregation?

THE PURPOSE OF REVIVAL

Revival is not just an "event." It is the supernatural working of God through His Holy Spirit where people are brought to Christ and changed by Him. As people are drawn into a confident relationship with Christ, they manifest the fullness of His life and demonstrate the richness of His power. True supernatural ministry at work in the Church begets vital, spiritually functional people throughout the whole church family.

Glorifying God is the Holy Spirit's intent in revival. As churches are revived and cities transformed by the mighty workings of the Holy Spirit, all the glory will be given back to the Father. To those consumed with a passion to know God and give all the glory to Him, He will manifest the glory of His person, His power, and His presence.

THE KEY TO REVIVAL

Revivals are birthed and maintained through prayer. Revival praying is rooted in confession of our sins and the sins of those people for whom we are interceding. As we pray, God forgives unrighteous attitudes, thought patterns, and actions that have hindered our relationship with Him. As we acknowledge God's power and sovereign lordship, God releases on earth what He has planned in heaven.

◇ What is the key for releasing God's purposes on earth? (Matt. 6:9, 10)

◇ Go back to the classic blueprint for how to lead a prayer revival in 2 Chronicles 7:14. What does God encourage us to do?

_____

_____

WORSHIP STARTS WITH ME

Leading people to and through revival calls us to our ultimate priority—to worship God. All ministry needs to be the natural out-flow of an intimate relationship with God, for it is He alone who imparts life, healing, forgiveness, and cleansing.

There is a worship pattern in the Old Testament that can help us visualize how ministry flows from the spiritual leader to the peo-ple. In Ezekiel 44:15–19, the priests were to worship God in the inner court of the temple, (representing ministry to the Lord); then receive God's enablement to minister in the outer court (represent-ing ministry to the people).

The God-given pattern in this text calls us to:

1. *Come near.* Put God at the center of your life every day. Draw close to Him.

2. *Minister to God.* Give Him the glory, honor, and power that are due Him.

3. *Stand before Him.* Wait upon God, be totally available to Him, and acknowledge His lordship.

◇ Explain why it is necessary for the spiritual leader to follow these three steps in his or her personal life before stepping forward to minister to others.

_____

FAITH ALIVE

◇ How will worshiping God as your first priority give you the resources you need to minister to others?

_____

◇ In what ways can you prepare for personal revival through prayer and worship?

_____

_____

◇ How can you communicate this to others?

_____

_____

REVIVAL DEMONSTRATES THE GOSPEL

◇ The apostle Paul was careful to point out that his preaching was not based on human wisdom. Instead, it was done in the "demonstration of the Spirit and of power" (1 Cor. 2:4). In the next verse, Paul contrasts effective and ineffective faith. In order for our faith to be authentic and powerful, in what does it need to be rooted?

_____

_____

KINGDOM EXTRA

Paul speaks of an apostolic priority that leadership must contend for in an era when the intellect is often deified and the demonstration of the Spirit and power either unsought or ridiculed. In 1 Corinthians 2:4, the word "demonstration" (Gr. *apodeixis*) is derived from the term used to describe actions that "exhibit or accredit, validate" a claim, a truth, or a presence. The New Testament apostolic value system sought and was grateful for the Holy Spirit's power-works. Therefore their manifestation is a worthy pursuit and expectation today as we declare God's Word or testify to the lost.

◇ After Christ was received up into heaven, His followers went out and "preached everywhere." Turn to Mark 16:20. What two things were happening simultaneously as they did this?

_____

_____

It is important to point out from this verse that the signs that accompanied the preaching of the word confirmed the word. Let's study the Word Wealth definition of "confirming."

WORD WEALTH

Confirming, *bebaioo* (Mark 16:20). To make firm, establish, secure, corroborate, guarantee. The miracles that accompanied the disciples' preaching confirmed to the people that the messengers were telling the truth, that God was backing up their message with supernatural phenomena, and that a new dispensation, the age of grace, had entered the world.

◇ What did the Lord commission His followers to do? (Mark 16:15)

_____

_____

◇ What specific signs follow those who believe? (vv. 17, 18)

_____

_____

◇ Explain the purpose of confirming signs. (v. 20)

_____

_____

EVANGELISM AND REVIVAL

In the New Testament, evangelism often followed demonstrations of God's kingdom power. For each of these events in Acts, write who came to the Lord and how God demonstrated His power.

Acts 5:12–15 _____

_____

Who believed: _____

_____

Evidence of God's power: _____

_____

_____

Acts 9:32–35

Who believed:

Evidence of God's power:

Acts 9:36–42

Who believed:

Evidence of God's power:

Acts 13:4–12

Who believed:

Evidence of God's power:

Acts 19:11–20

Who believed:

Evidence of God's power:

Faith in the power of God (1 Cor. 2:1–5; 4:20) or "power evangelism" does not diminish the importance of preaching about sin, the Cross, or Christ's Resurrection. It does affirm that often people's hearts are opened to a spiritually sensitive leader when they see God act. Once their hearts are opened, a spiritually sensitive leader can more fully instruct them (Acts 18:24–26). As we are available to be used by God in this way, we need to be aware that the words and works of God function together.

◈ Explain the relationship of Jesus' words to His works. (John 14:10, 11)

_____

_____

_____

_____

◈ Do powerful works of God convince everyone of the truth of the gospel? (Matt. 11:20–24)

_____

_____

FAITH ALIVE

◈ How can leaders teach people to avoid the tragic mistake of "using" God to "make" Him act for the sake of show or sensation?

_____

_____

◈ Expect manifestations of the Holy Spirit through your ministry. Ask the Lord to validate the glory of the gospel with His power.

_____

_____

GUIDELINES AMID A VISITATION OF GOD

We have seen that there is no better example of revival than in the Book of Acts. As Jesus' followers spread the word of the gospel and the Spirit confirmed the word with power, revival broke out. So explosive was this revival, it was as if the world had turned "upside down" (Acts 17:6).

When God moves powerfully, the wise leader will handle this "explosiveness" with care. There are five basic steps a spiritual leader can take to ensure that people truly glorify God in the midst of powerful revival.

For each of the five guidelines, choose one of these exercises:

(a) Write what the scriptures say about that particular guideline or:

(b) Write practical ideas on how to implement these guidelines into your ministry or into the ministries of those you will lead.

1. Follow the life of the Holy Spirit. If we respond to the revival in fear (quenching the Spirit) or presumption (seizing initiative God hasn't given us), we grieve the Holy Spirit. (See Eph. 4:30; 5:18; 1 Thess. 5:19)

---

2. Resolve not to "control" the revival. Seek God for discernment between "leading" and "restricting"; monitor the visitation, but stay submitted to Him. Give wise stewardship to the gracious move of the Spirit. (See 1 Cor. 4:1, 2; James 4:7; 1 Pet. 2:21)

---

3. Seek the counsel of gifted ministries, each submitting to and complementing the other as God has designed His church to work together. (See Prov. 11:14; 1 Cor. 12:1–28; 14:32; Eph. 4:11, 12; 1 Thess. 5:11)

---

4. Always complement the experiential side of the visitation with the consistent, systematic teaching of the Word of God. (See Luke 24:27; Acts 17:11; Eph. 6:17; Heb. 4:12)

---

5. Always keep the focus of the revival on God, not "things that happen." In a genuine move of God, people will need to be led to worship God and glorify Him as the Initiator and Sustainer of such

blessing, and the Source of wisdom and power to walk wisely in it. (See Acts 2:42–47; Acts 9:36–43; Acts 19:11–20)

_____

_____

_____

GUARD AGAINST DWINDLING FIRES

Picture this circumstance: God is doing powerful things. Revival is here. People are coming to the Lord, miracles are happening. Is there anything a spiritual leader can do to make sure the fires of revival don't diminish?

It is important to realize that revival fires wane for various reasons. Sometimes the purposes of God have been fulfilled as believers have been quickened to evangelism and new outreaches have been birthed. If this is the case, the Lord will guide leadership on ways to carry out His purposes for this next exciting season of growth.

Other times, genuine revival can be cut short and the fire of the Holy Spirit quenched through unrealized compromise. It is important that the leader take steps to guard against the "dwindling fires" of Holy-Spirit led revival.

Like water eroding a riverbank, the following situations have the potential to undermine the effectiveness and power of genuine revival in the church. The wise spiritual leader will exercise vigilance to guard against these signs of dwindling revival fires:

1. The excitement of crowds and miracles dulls our ears to hearing the foundational truths of the Holy Spirit's counsel.

2. We look to the visitation of the Spirit to shore up weaknesses in the local fellowship rather than correct problems.

3. An attitude of pride and showmanship distorts the simplicity of God's workings, and the visitation is reduced to a cleverly publicized event.

4. We fail to maintain the balance of the pastoral needs of the congregation, substituting the sheer energy of the meetings for shepherd care and faithful feeding of the sheep.

5. We don't train disciples who would have multiplied the effectiveness of the revival.

6. The authority and unity in the leadership team breaks down through prayerlessness, weariness, or functioning outside the boundaries of individuals' giftings.

7. We look to "professionals" to further the growth of the church instead of fostering the release of ministries that have bonded to the life and value system of the congregation.

8. We lose the focus and object of loving worship by using "worship" as a means of stimulating desired responses in people.

9. The "busyness and excitement" of revival takes priority over vigilance in humble prayer and intercession.

10. We see revival as a way to advance a private local "kingdom" (congregation), rather than to benefit the whole body of Christ (John 12:24).

 FAITH ALIVE

⬥ Study these ten warning signals with a positive perspective. Rather than applying them to criticize any situations you have seen, seek to discern how a wise leader can avoid these pitfalls.

_____

_____

Now choose at least one to study in depth. Write down: What has gone wrong in this situation?

⬥ How the leader can guide people away from this error and into healthy truth.

_____

_____

⬥ What scriptures deal with this situation.

_____

_____

◇ How the leader can encourage people to want God's best for their lives.

_____

_____

HANG IN THERE

The passion for God to move among His people sometimes seems slow in being rewarded. Sincere leaders often labor, pray, and seek fruitfulness for extended seasons before the visitation of God's grace brings the long-sought harvest.

◇ Many faithful leaders throughout the years have found great comfort in the promise of Galatians 6:9. What is the promise?

_____

_____

◇ When we feel that we are laboring with no apparent result, what is our encouragement? (1 Cor. 15:58)

_____

_____

God's call to the earnest leader or congregation is, *Do not lose heart; harvest is certain.* Spirit-directed words, actions, giving, serving, and loving are all good seeds. God has promised to multiply those good seeds back to you. There is a due season—wait for it.

FAITH ALIVE

Ask the Lord how you can prepare for His refreshing and revival. Take extra time this week just to listen to His voice. Write down the thoughts He gives you.

_____

_____

MIRACLES, SIGNS, AND WONDERS

Lesson 9

THE BIG IDEA

There is increasing evidence of God's readiness to move supernaturally in our world through divine visitations of His grace. From the increased number of souls being saved to manifestations of miracles, signs, and wonders, God invites us: "Call to Me, and I will answer you, and show you great and mighty things, which you do not know" (Jer. 33:3).

MIRACLES AMONG US

The miraculous is demonstrated throughout the entire Bible—from Genesis, which deals with creation, to Revelation, which deals with the Coming of the Lord and the new creation. In the New Testament, the miracle of Jesus' conception by the Holy Spirit in the womb of a virgin named Mary was a sign that God is "with us." Following His birth and the supernatural signs that accompanied it (Luke 2:8–14), the four Gospels recorded the miracles performed by Christ. Miracles, signs, and wonders didn't stop after His Crucifixion. These manifestations of God's power accompanied the ministry and preaching of the early church leaders, continued throughout the history of the church, and are present in the church today.

◇ What sign prophesied in Isaiah 7:14 was fulfilled in Luke 1:31? What was the significance of that sign?

_____

_____

◇ What three things were characteristic of Jesus' ministry? (Acts 2:22)

_____

◈ Where did these signs, miracles, and wonders take place?
(v. 22)

_____

_____

_____

THE MIRACULOUS DEFINED

Miracles are "historic events or natural phenomena which appear to violate or transcend natural laws but which reveal God to the eye of faith at the same time. A helpful way of understanding the meaning of miracles is to examine the various terms for miracles used in the Bible. Both the Old Testament and the New Testament use the word *sign* (Is. 7:11, 14; John 2:11) to denote a miracle that points to a deeper revelation. *Wonder* (Joel 2:30; Mark 13:22) emphasizes the effect of the miracle, causing awe and even terror. A *work* (Matt. 11:2) points to the presence of God in history, acting for mankind. The New Testament uses the word *power* (Mark 6:7) to emphasize God's acting in strength. These terms often overlap in meaning (Acts 2:43). They are more specific than the more general term *miracle*."[4]

A sign is "something that points to, or represents, something larger or more important than itself. The word is used in this way to refer to a wide variety of things in the Bible. But by far the most important use of the word is in reference to the acts of God. Thus, it is often linked with *wonders*. In the Old Testament most references point to the miracles produced by God to help deliver the Hebrew people from slavery in Egypt (Ex. 7:3; Is. 8:18). In the New Testament the word *signs* is linked with both *wonders* and *miracles* (Acts 2:22; 2 Cor. 12:12; Heb. 2:4). Signs point primarily to the powerful, saving activity of God as experienced through the ministry of Jesus and the apostles. The word occurs frequently in the Gospel of John, pointing to the deeper, symbolic meaning of the miracles performed by Jesus. Throughout the Bible the true significance of a sign is understood only through faith."[5]

WORD WEALTH

To gain more insight, study how these Word Wealth power words were used in the biblical Greek.

Signs, *semeion* (Rev. 16:14). A sign, mark, token. The word is used to distinguish between persons or objects (Matt. 26:48; Luke 2:12); to denote a warning or admonition (Matt. 12:39; 16:4); as an omen portending future events (Mark 13:4; Luke 21:7); to describe miracles and wonders, whether indicating divine authority (Matt. 12:38, 39; Mark 8:11, 12) or ascribed to false teachers and demons (Matt. 24:24; Rev. 16:14).

Wonders, *teras* (Acts 15:12). Compare "teratology," the science that deals with unexplainable phenomena. *Teras* denotes extraordinary occurrences, supernatural prodigies, omens, portents, unusual manifestations, miraculous incidents portending the future rather than the past, and acts that are so unusual they cause the observer to marvel or be in awe. *Teras* is always in the plural, associated with *semeion* (signs). Signs and wonders are a perfect balance for touching man's intellect, emotions, and will.

◇ What does Daniel 4:3 say about signs and wonders? Daniel 6:27?

_____

_____

◇ Define miracles, signs, and wonders.

_____

_____

◇ In what way do miracles, signs, and wonders point the way to God?

_____

_____

_____

THE MIRACLES OF CHRIST

Miracles and supernatural phenomena were a part of Christ's ministry. All four Gospel writers speak of at least thirty-seven miracles that He performed. In addition, the Book of John says that Christ did so many things that "the world itself could not contain the books that would be written" (21:25). In His wisdom, the Holy Spirit included those miracles that would best serve His church in the Gospels. Take a look at three of them.

◇ Calming the Storm (Mark 4:35–41)

What was the miracle?

What effect did the miracle have?

◇ The Demon-possessed Healed (Matt. 8:28–34)

What was the miracle?

What effect did the miracle have?

◇ Miraculous Catch of Fish (Luke 5:1–11)

What was the miracle?

What effect did the miracle have?

FAITH ALIVE

Focus on the miracle of Jesus calming the storm. How do you react when you are experiencing a circumstantial storm? Does it sometimes seem to you that the Lord is unavailable? As you ponder the power of God, what encouragement does this miracle give you?

KINGDOM EXTRA

Other miracles Jesus performed in the Gospels include healing (Matt. 8:14; Mark 1:31), raising the dead (Luke 7:11; John 11), feeding five thousand people with a few loaves and fishes (John 6:5), walking on the water (Matt. 14:26, 27), casting out devils (Matt. 12:22), cleansing lepers (Matt. 8:3), and opening blind eyes and deaf ears (Matt. 9:27; Mark 7:37).

The Old Testament is replete with the supernatural workings of God. An excellent case study is God's dealings through Moses in Exodus: (1) Moses' call and preparation (3:1—4:9); (2) signs and wonders preceding their release from Egyptian bondage (7:14—11:10); (3) the Passover instituted (12:1–51); (4) the crossing of the

Red Sea (14:1–31); (5) miraculous provision of food and water (15:22;17:6). In addition, the Old Testament records many miracles that took place under spiritual leaders. Some of these are Joshua (Josh. 3—11); Samuel (1 Sam. 12:18); Elijah (1 Kin. 17:1–24); Elisha (2 Kin. 2:14—6:17); Isaiah (2 Kin. 20:1–11).

THE PURPOSE OF THE MIRACULOUS

Whether in the Old Testament, or in the New, the purpose of all miracles, signs, and wonders is that people might experience the reality and power of God. Let's study how Jesus taught this through the Great Commission.

◇ What are Jesus' followers to do? (Mark 16:15, 16)

◇ What signs will follow those who believe? (vv. 17, 18)

◇ What happened to Jesus after He talked to His disciples? (v. 19)

Verse twenty highlights the purpose of God regarding the miraculous by saying that as His followers went out to preach, the Lord was "confirming the Word through the accompanying signs." Signs accompany the preaching of the Word by lending authenticity to the message as the Word Wealth suggests.

WORD WEALTH

Confirming, *bebaioo* (Mark 16:20). To make firm, establish, secure, corroborate, guarantee. The miracles that accompanied the disciples' preaching confirmed to the people that the messengers were telling the truth, that God was backing up their message with supernatural phenomena, and that a new dispensation, the age of grace, had entered the world.

◇ Who corroborates the Word through signs? What does this signify? (16:20)

_____

_____

◇ Did the apostles follow through with Jesus' instructions to confirm the Word with accompanying signs? (Acts 5:12)

_____

_____

◇ How does Acts 5:12 describe the people's cohesiveness as a group?

_____

_____

Miracles themselves do not bring salvation, but they often attract people to the message. The miracles of the Bible are "signs," in that they convey important spiritual messages and confirm the veracity of the Word of the gospel.

FAITH ALIVE

What do you understand to be the purpose of miracles, signs, and wonders? What is their significance to your life? To your leadership?

THE MIRACULOUS IN THE EARLY CHURCH

Miracles, signs and wonders were commonly accepted in the early church, and spiritual leaders led the way in giving place to such ministry. They did not see God's supernatural movings as random, occasional events. Rather, signs, miracles, and wonders were welcomed as worthy evidences of God's anointing continually glorifying Christ through the church.

◇ The unbelieving "religious" leaders did concede that a "notable miracle" had been done through Peter. What was that miracle? (Acts 3:1–10)

_____

_____

◇ What was the significance of this healing? (vv. 12–16)

_____

_____

◇ What was the result of this healing? (Acts 4:4)

_____

_____

◇ When threatened, what did the early church leaders pray for? (Acts 4:29, 30)

_____

_____

◇ What did God do in response to their prayer? (v. 31)

_____

_____

◇ Peter, Paul, and others in the New Testament powerfully demonstrated the fulfillment of Jesus' promise of signs following. For each reference for Peter and Paul, write what the miracle was and the effect it had upon the people.

1. Miracles through Peter

   Acts 5:15 _____

   _____

   Acts 9:34 _____

   _____

2. Miracles through Paul

   Acts 13:11, 12 _____

   _____

   Acts 14:8–10 _____

   _____

   Acts 16:16–18 _____

   _____

3. Miracles through others: Others in the New Testament experienced miracles, such as the seventy (Luke 10:17–19), Stephen (Acts 6:8), Philip (Acts 8:6–13), and Barnabas and Paul (Acts 15:12). In the early church, the Lord distributed spiritual gifts such as healings and working of miracles (1 Cor. 12:8–10).

◈ Why do you think the Lord gave His followers the supernatural power to perform signs?

_____

_____

◈ Is there a need today for similar signs?

_____

_____

_____

FIVE PRINCIPLES FOR BALANCE

As powerful and miraculous events pervaded the early church, the people followed certain principles showing balance in their approach to the miraculous.

◈ Turn to Acts 8:4–40. For each principle, write the event that was taking place.

1. A central focus is on God's Word and the glory of God and His Son Jesus. (Acts 8:4, 5, 35)

_____

2. There are confirming signs of evangelism, healing, and deliverance. (vv. 6, 7, 9–13, 25)

_____

3. A spirit of "joy" prevails, contrasted with mere crowd excitement or sensationalism. (v. 8)

_____

4. Basics of sound discipleship are set in place through required water baptism (vv. 12; 36–38), with follow-up ministry of the baptism with the Holy Spirit. (vv. 14–17)

_____

5. When satanic intrusion attempts to pollute any move of God, wise and confrontive leadership will block the enemy's efforts. (vv. 18–24)

While God's mighty works transcend the normal human condition and exceed human powers of accomplishment, New Testament leaders did not pander to a carnal following after sensationalism in the early church. Likewise, today the quest for supernatural life and ministry needs to be pursued, but on biblical grounds and with spiritually balanced wisdom.

FAITH ALIVE

How can you seek to find balance while contending for the miraculous through your ministry?

In an age of false doctrines and misguided practices concerning the supernatural, what is the value of spiritual discernment in determining the true source of miracles?

MIRACLES TODAY

Miracles, signs, and wonders were realities to the people in the Bible who experienced them. Miraculous events accompanied the ministry and preaching of early church leaders, and there are no scriptures that indicate that these were to be discontinued. Instead, miracles are presented in the New Testament as legitimate, credible, and desirable assets for spiritual leadership today.

◈ Wonders and signs are not an exclusive characteristic of apostolic ministry. Let's look at Stephen. He was not an apostle (Acts 6:1–6), but was graced with what two things? (Acts 6:8).

◈ What did God empower Stephen to do among the people? (6:8)

◇ Philip was another "non-apostle" like Stephen, but that was no hindrance to his miracle ministry. What were the miracles? (Acts 8:7)

_____

_____

◇ Among whom does God work miracles? (Gal. 3:5)

_____

_____

We read in Mark 16:15–18 that attesting signs would accompany those who believed in Jesus. Indeed, all the signs listed in that passage have occurred repeatedly in Christian history. Signs accredit the gospel message and cannot be limited to the apostolic age, any more than the Lord's commission to carry the gospel throughout the world. The signs, therefore, confirm the ministries of Christ's ambassadors in every generation. Casting out demons, speaking in tongues, and healing all appear in other passages in the New Testament, and there is no scriptural warrant for their cessation before the Lord returns.

FAITH ALIVE

What is the norm for the Spirit-filled, Spirit-led church?

How can you prepare your heart to embrace the miraculous working of God through your ministry and in the ministries of those you will lead?

DREAMS AND VISIONS
Lesson 10

THE BIG IDEA

With the birth of the church came the assurance that people would experience God-given visions and dreams as His Spirit was poured out upon them. What does this mean? Are dreams and visions for today? How do Life-giving leaders approach the supernatural works of God with balanced perspective?

DREAMS AND VISIONS PROPHESIED

But this is what was spoken by the prophet Joel: "And it shall come to pass in the last days, says God, that I will pour out of My Spirit on all flesh; your sons and your daughters shall prophesy, your young men shall see visions, your old men shall dream dreams. And on My menservants and on My maidservants I will pour out My Spirit in those days; and they shall prophesy." (Acts 2:16–18)

People were praying, seeking, believing. Then suddenly the Holy Spirit was poured out on them. This outpouring, predicted in Joel's messianic word, was a sign that Jesus had been exalted to the Father and that He was breathing life into His body—His church. In the midst of this, Peter stood up to communicate what was happening. Visions, dreams, prophecies—how could these be? The text we just read is Peter's explanation.

◈ Compare the part of Peter's sermon that corresponds with Joel's prophetic word (Acts 2:17–21; Joel 2:28–32). What are the three evidences of the Spirit's outpouring found in both texts?

_____

_____

◈ Why do you think these three signs are mentioned?

_____

When are these signs to take place? (Acts 2:17). Note that this term refers to the era of the church from Pentecost to the return of Christ. (See Heb. 1:1, 2).

◇ Peter made it clear that the coming of the Spirit was not just for themselves (the apostles and their contemporaries) but for others also. To whom is the promise given? What are the implications of that promise for today's believer? (Acts 2:38, 39)

It is important that we possess the conviction that the *promise* of the Holy Spirit is a gift for every believer in every generation. *All who are afar off* includes Gentiles. Peter's words clearly extend to every believer in every era and everywhere. We have full reason to expect the same resource and experience that was afforded the first believers who received the Holy Spirit at the birth of the church. (See Acts 1:4, 5; 2:33; Luke 24:49; Is. 57:19; Eph. 2:13, 17.)

FAITH ALIVE

If dreams and visions were prophesied in the Old Testament, present at the birth of the church and promised to all believers, then this is a subject well worth your re-examination as a leader. Ask the Lord to speak to you in a fresh way as you study.

COUNTERFEIT VS. THE REAL THING

Our culture's perception of dreams and visions has become so twisted, it is important to fully understand what the Bible has to say about them. Unlike the world, we are not to seek after dreams and visions through some type of quest. However, as we seek God through Jesus Christ, dreams and visions can happen as a by-product of the Holy Spirit moving in and through us.

God-given dreams and visions always confirm His Word. Let's see how the Bible defines them.

WORD WEALTH

Dreams, *chalom* (Joel 2:28). A dream; a vision in the night. The root of this noun is the verb *chalam*, "to dream." Dreams of various types are mentioned in Scripture, ranging from the product of one's imagination to the vehicle of God's communication with a person (compare Eccl. 5:3 and Gen. 20:6). Many biblical figures, such as Jacob, Laban, Pharaoh, Solomon, and Nebuchadnezzar are known for having dreams (see 1 Kin. 3:5; Dan. 2:1). Joseph and Daniel are the biblical champions of dream-revelation; each not only received his own dreams but also interpreted the dreams of others as well.

◈ Who appeared in Solomon's dream at Gibeon? (1 Kin. 3:5)

_____

_____

◈ Why do you think God would choose to communicate through a dream?

_____

_____

Visions are "experiences similar to dreams through which supernatural insight or awareness is given by revelation. The difference between a dream and a vision is that dreams occur only during sleep, while visions can happen while a person is awake (Dan. 10:7).

In the Bible, people who had visions were filled with a special consciousness of God. The most noteworthy Old Testament examples of recipients of visions are Ezekiel and Daniel. Visions in the New Testament are most prominent in the Gospel of Luke, the Book of Acts, and the Book of Revelation. The Holy Spirit's use of this means of personal prompting was prophesied by Joel (2:28–32) and affirmed at the birth of the church to be an abiding operation of the Holy Spirit's dealings with believers. Visions never supercede Scripture, but like dreams and prophecies, are to be tested by the Word (2 Pet. 1:16–21) and judged (1 Cor. 14:29)—that is, evaluated by mature believers." [6]

◈ What are the differences between visions and dreams? The similarities?

_____

_____

◈ Look up 2 Peter 1:16–21 and 1 Corinthians 14:29. Why is it essential to test every vision or dream?

_____

_____

NEW TESTAMENT EXAMPLES

The New Testament opens with a burst of dreams, visions, angelic visitations, and prophecies and closes with John's revelation on the isle of Patmos. Throughout, there are many encounters with God in dreams and visions. Yet, neither Jesus nor the apostles give any particular precept concerning the phenomena of dreams or visions. This is somewhat enigmatic in that, while the Bible does not teach about dreams and visions in any systematic manner, citing so many significant examples validates their existence and use by God as a means of communicating to people.

◇ Profound things happened as each person responded to a God-given vision or dream. Write the message and the result of the dream or vision.

Persons Involved	Scripture	Message of Dream/Vision	Result of Dream/Vision
The wisemen	Matthew 2:12		
Joseph's first dream	Matthew 1:20–23		
Joseph's second dream	Matthew 2:13–15		
Joseph's third and fourth	Matthew 2:19–23		
Cornelius	Acts 10:3–8		
Peter	Acts 10:9–24, 34, 43–48		
Ananias	Acts 9:10–18		
Paul	Acts 16:9, 10		
Paul	Acts 18:9–11		

◇ In giving his testimony to King Agrippa, Paul says he was not disobedient to the _____ (Acts 26:19). What do you think this means?

_____

_____

◇ Apparently Paul was given powerful visions and revelations which he described in 2 Corinthians 12:1–4. What was Paul's attitude of heart regarding these things? (vv. 5–9)

_____

_____

◇ Supernatural revelation always involves alignment to the word of _____ and to the testimony of _____. (Rev. 1:1, 2). This means that while God may guide through supernatural means, all such special guidance must be grounded in the unchanging revelation of the Bible.

FAITH ALIVE

Think about what would have happened if people hadn't paid attention to their visions or dreams at key points of biblical history. For instance, what would have happened if:

1. Joseph hadn't protected the young Child, Jesus, by taking Him to Egypt?

2. Ananias hadn't ministered to Saul of Tarsus?

3. Peter had disobeyed the message of his vision to minister to the Gentiles?

◇ Where would we be as a church? Where would you be as a believer?

_____

_____

_____

_____

_____

_____

PROPHETIC VISION IN THE OLD TESTAMENT

Dreams and visions were the common ways in which prophecy came in Old Testament times. The prophets understood God's counsels so clearly because He revealed matters to them by visible means.

KINGDOM EXTRA

One word for vision in the Hebrew, *chazon*, occurs 35 times and is from the root *chazah*, "to see, behold, and perceive." *Chazon* is especially used for the divine revelation of truth which the prophets received. For further study, see Isaiah 1:1; Ezekiel 12:27, 28; Daniel 8:1, 2; Obadiah 1; Habakkuk 2:2, 3.

The coming of the Messiah was a huge truth that God revealed prophetically in a *chazon* vision to Isaiah (1:1). This prophet did not imagine these things in his own mind; God showed them to him and anointed him to write them down. His visions provide a textbook outline of the gospel:

1. the virgin shall conceive (7:14)
2. a Child is born, a Son is given (9:6)
3. the ministry of Jesus (61:1–3)
4. the Crucifixion (52:13—53:12)
5. Gentiles are redeemed by the Lord (60:1–3)
6. the Redeemer's glorious return (63:1–5; 64:1–5)
7. the new heaven and earth (66:22)

Using a concordance or annotated notes in your Bible, find the place in the New Testament where each of these prophecies was fulfilled.

CASE STUDIES FROM THE OLD TESTAMENT

God spoke through dreams and visions in the Old Testament to give direction or to communicate a message. Jacob and Joseph are two patriarchs who received a "visual message" from God.

Jacob's dream gave him a glimpse into the heavenly world. The dream emphasized God's initiating grace as He assured Jacob that He is the Lord of the past and future. Turn to this dream in Genesis 28:12–16.

◇ What picture did Jacob see in the dream? (v. 12)

_____

_____

◇ All dreams and visions from God turn our eyes to Him. In this dream, why is it significant that the Lord was standing above the ladder? (v. 13)

_____

_____

◇ How did God identify Himself? (v. 13)

_____

_____

◇ What promise did God give to Jacob? (vv. 13–15)

_____

_____

◇ How did Jacob's promise confirm the word of the Lord given to Abraham in a vision? (Gen. 15:1–6)

_____

_____

◇ How do you know that Jacob's dream moved him to a new consecration to God? (Gen. 28:16–22)

_____

_____

Joseph's dreams gave him insight into future events. These events would occur not only in his life, but also in his family and country.

1. Joseph Dreams of Exaltation (Gen. 37:5–9)

◇ Joseph had two unusual prophetic dreams that did not gain him popularity in his family. Describe the first dream. (Gen. 37:5–7)

_____

_____

◇ What emotion did Joseph's brothers have when he told them his dream? (v. 5)

_____

◇ Relate the second dream. What bowed down to Joseph? (v. 9)

_____

◇ How did Joseph's father respond to this dream? (vv. 10, 11)

_____

◇ As Joseph told his dreams, how do you think he did it? Was he cocky, flaunting his "favored son" status, or was he just naive? (vv. 3, 4)

_____

_____

◇ Do you think Joseph understood the depth of the prophetic nature of the dreams? Was he wise in sharing them with his family when he did?

_____

_____

Joseph's two dreams of exaltation did come to pass, but his life took several odd turns before the fulfillment came:

1. His angry, jealous brothers seized him and sold him into slavery (Gen. 37:23–28).

2. Joseph was taken to Egypt and became a successful overseer for an officer of Pharaoh (39:1–6).

3. Joseph was thrown into prison on a false charge (39:7–20).

4. After all was said and done, Joseph was given a high position in Egypt and his brothers did indeed humbly bow before him—just as he had predicted in his prophetic dream (Gen. 42:6).

◇ The psalmist summarizes Joseph's experience in Psalm 105:17–22. What had to happen before Joseph was released from the painful fetters and irons that held him captive? (vv. 18, 19)

_____

_____

_____

_____

_____

◇ How was Joseph changed by his hardships?

_____

_____

_____

_____

_____

FAITH ALIVE

What have you learned from Joseph's story about the wisdom of sharing your dreams too soon?

Has God given you a dream that seems long in coming? The best thing to do is to wait upon Him. If the dream is from God, it will be fulfilled, not from your own energy but in His timing and plan.

2. Joseph interprets dreams in prison (Gen. 40:5–23)

◇ Two of Pharaoh's officers who had been imprisoned had a dream that troubled them. What was the chief butler's dream and its interpretation? (v. 9–13)

_____

_____

◇ What was the chief baker's dream and its interpretation? (vv. 16–19)

_____

_____

◇ What happened to the butler and baker that confirmed the truth that God gave to Joseph? (20–22)

_____

_____

◇ To whom did Joseph give the credit for the true interpretation of dreams? (v. 8)

_____

_____

3. Joseph interprets Pharaoh's dream (Gen. 41:1–36)

When Pharaoh heard that God had given Joseph the correct interpretation of the baker's dream and the butler's dream, he sent for Joseph to interpret his own frightening dreams (41:14, 15). Joseph was released and ultimately given the highest office in Egypt because Pharaoh recognized the wisdom of God in him (41:39–44).

◇ What were Pharaoh's dreams? (41:1–7, 15–24)

_____

_____

◇ Why couldn't the magicians interpret Pharaoh's dreams? (v. 8)

_____

_____

_____

◇ What was the interpretation of Pharaoh's dreams? (vv. 25–32)

_____

◇ What practical benefit was derived from Joseph's interpretation of Pharaoh's dreams? (vv. 33–36)

_____

_____

◇ Describe the events that confirmed the truth of God's message through the dream. (vv. 47–49, 53–57)

_____

_____

◇ The famine was so severe that all the surrounding countries came to acquire grain (41:57), including Joseph's brothers who "bowed down before him" (42:6). How was this a fulfillment of Joseph's original dreams in 37:7–9?

_____

_____

_____

◇ Joseph said repeatedly that God was to get the glory for the interpretations given him. Write how this was communicated in each of these verses and tell how this reflects a change in Joseph's attitude.

40:8 _____

_____

41:16 _____

_____

41:38, 39 _____

_____

FAITH ALIVE

Joseph resisted pride when he prefaced the interpretation of Pharaoh's dreams by giving glory to God. Tell of an occasion in your own life when you were able to give God glory for ministering through you.

MORE TO COME

There is much to be said about this subject in the next chapter. What do you do with dreams and visions when God gives them? Should dreams and visions be tested? How does a Life-giving leader encourage people to receive them with balance and soundness of faith? How can a leader be inspired to fully trust in God's plan through the vision or dream God has given them?

YOUR DREAMS AND VISIONS

Lesson 11

THE BIG IDEA

Leaders are people of prophetic vision who have a heart to receive and believe that God-given dreams are possibilities.

Gideon was afraid. God had told him to take a small army and fight against their enemies. At God's direction, Gideon approached the camp of the enemy and overheard a man telling his companion his dream. It was through this dream and its interpretation that God gave Gideon the courage to follow through with His plan for victory. This story is told in Judges 7:9–15.

◇ What three images describe the size of Israel's army in Judges 7:12?

_____

_____

◇ What did God tell Gideon to do? Why do you think God told him to do this? (vv. 10, 11)

_____

_____

◇ Tell the content and the interpretation of the dream that Gideon overheard. (vv. 13, 14)

_____

_____

The barley bread in this dream symbolized Israel, which appeared to be inferior and smaller than the Midianite army. (Barley was considered an inferior grain that was used by the poor.) When the barley loaf struck the enemy's tent and collapsed it, God was giving a symbolic message that victory was assured.

◇ What did Gideon do *first* after he heard the dream and its interpretation? (v. 15)

_____

_____

◇ How did this dream turn Gideon's eyes from seeing the problem to visualizing God's solution? What happened as a result? (vv. 15–25)

_____

_____

So remarkable was Gideon's triumph that the Book of Hebrews mentions him as one of the "heroes" of faith (Heb. 11:32).

FAITH ALIVE

Through a dream, the Lord was gracious to tell Gideon what to do to conquer his fear—worship God and believe His Word that He would grant victory. How does redirecting your focus to God through worship and faith in His Word help you conquer your fears?

SIX PURPOSES OF DREAMS

A dream gave Gideon the encouragement he needed to cast aside his doubts and pursue the victory. There are six other things that dreams from God can do:

Dreams:

1. Provide God's answers to our questions (see Judg. 7:10–15).
2. Instruct us in the things of God (see Matt. 1:19–21).
3. Warn us about unseen dangers (see Matt. 2:12, 22).
4. Guide us away from wrongdoing (see Gen. 20:3–8; 31:24; Matt. 27:19).
5. Keep us from pride (see Dan. 4:19–37).
6. Save our lives (see Matt. 2:13).

◇ Look up the cross-references and describe how those situations demonstrate the principle.

_____

God's Word to me:	I am encouraged to:	My plan of action:
"I will stand my watch" (2:1)	Meet with the Lord regularly in a special place of prayer	
I will "watch to see" (2:1)	Look for God to speak to you in dreams and visions	
"He will say to me" (2:1)	Listen for the word of the Lord	
"Write the vision" (2:2)	Keep a journal of things that God says	
"Though it tarries, wait for it . . . it will surely come" (2:3)	Wait for God to bring it to pass	

EMBRACE THE VISION

The presence of vision creates hope and brings change when articulated with enthusiasm. One of the most inspiring accounts in the Bible about spiritual vision comes through the prophet Habakkuk.

Read Habakkuk 2:1–3, taking time to process what is said. You will note that the passage begins with the prophet watching and waiting to see what the Lord is going to say to him. Then comes God's answer—He imparts vision and tells Habakkuk what to do with it.

FAITH ALIVE

You, too, can follow the example of the prophet and pursue the vision God gives you. Take a look at the chart. For each statement from God's Word, there is a corresponding reassurance that comes to you from the heart of God. Take encouragement from this, pray over it, and write down how to apply each action into your life.

COMMUNICATE THE VISION

Every spiritual leader is concerned about how to impart his or her vision to others. This passage from Habakkuk gives an excellent outline on communicating vision.

◇ Focusing now on what is said about the vision, review the truths God imparted to Habakkuk. Write what God said next to each principle.

The vision:

1. Must be written: (2:2) "_____"

2. Must be clear: (2:2) "_____"

3. Must be motivating to those who read it: (2:2) "_____"

4. Has a time when it is to take place: (2:3) "_____"

5. Must be received with patience: (2:3) "_____"

6. Is often delayed: (2:3) "_____,"

7. But its fulfillment will be certain: (2:3) "_____"

Like the prophet Habakkuk, we can take a posture before God that enables us to hear His voice and communicate the vision He has given us.

WHEN THERE'S NO VISION

The presence or absence of vision will determine whether or not people become lethargic. Spiritual health wanes when there is no vision.

◇ When a society lacks revelation from God, what happens? (Prov. 29:18)

_____

_____

_____

_____

◇ 1 Samuel 3:1 describes a tragic condition: "The word of the LORD was rare in those days; there was no widespread revelation." But hope returns: "The LORD appeared again. . . . The LORD revealed Himself to Samuel." By what means was the Lord revealed? (3:21)

_____

_____

_____

The word *reveal* is important when it comes to prophetic revelation. Amos 3:7 says God "reveals His secret to His servants the prophets." The word *reveals* has the same root in the Hebrew as the verse you just read in 1 Samuel 3:21. Let's check out the Word Wealth definition.

WORD WEALTH

Reveals, *galah* (Amos 3:7). To uncover, reveal, open, lay bare, strip away, denude, expose, disclose, unveil; to depart, or to go into exile. In the present reference, *galah* has to do with the Lord's laying bare, exposing, revealing, uncovering, and disclosing His secret plans to the prophets, who are His servants.

◇ The New Testament says the "mystery [secret or hidden truth] which has been hidden from ages and from generations," has now been "revealed to His saints" (Col. 1:26). What is the mystery now revealed to us? (v. 27)

_____

_____

_____

_____

DOES THE BIBLE FORBID THE INTERPRETATION OF DREAMS AND VISIONS?

We know God reveals His plan through His Word. We have seen that God can, in certain circumstances, reveal His plan through a dream or vision. But is it scriptural to interpret a dream or vision, and if you do, what are the guidelines?

The Bible does not forbid the interpretation of dreams and visions; however, great caution needs to be exercised. We know that Scripture did record occasions when God spoke through a dream or vision (see Job 33:14–16; Acts 2:17). Joseph (Gen. 41:1–36), Daniel (Dan. 2:19–45) and Paul (Acts 16:9, 10) interpreted dreams and visions. The critical issue is the *source* of the dream. Some dreams come from God, some from within ourselves, and some from the realm of the demonic.

It is important to emphasize that the Bible forthrightly condemns dreams resulting from divination. Divination is the art or practice that seeks to foresee or foretell future events or discover hidden knowledge by the aid of demonic supernatural powers. The Bible forbids consulting persons who practice such arts (Deut. 18:10–12; see also 13:1–5). Therefore, those who lead need to help people avoid confusion as they seek answers in this area. The bottom line is that the interpretation of dreams and visions belongs to God (Gen. 40:8), and His Word of truth needs to be sought at all times.

◈ Look up Deuteronomy 13:1–5 and 18:10–12. What do these verses say about interpretations that are either false, demonic, or lead a person away from God?

_____

_____

_____

_____

_____

God indeed can reveal Himself to us in dreams and visions. This explains why false prophets rely upon counterfeit dreams and visions; it lends "so-called" credibility to their fraudulent messages.

TEST DREAMS AND VISIONS

When prophets, dreams, and visions are false, they lead people away from God, cultivating spiritual recklessness and moral irresponsibility (see Jer. 23:32). It is essential that a spiritual leader teach people to examine every Revelation to determine whether it is true or false. Think of a Revelation and answer the following questions.

Does the vision or dream reinforce God's Word and:

◇ Lead people to Christ and fill them with love for His church? If so, how?

_____

_____

◇ Align itself with the clear and complete teachings of the Bible? If so, how?

_____

_____

◇ Strengthen faith and give people an honorable purpose in life? If so, how?

_____

_____

◇ Turn people from wrongdoing, promoting righteousness and purity in their lives? If so, how?

_____

_____

◇ Find wide acceptance and affirmation by notable men and women of God? If so, how?

_____

_____

◇ Build up the body of Christ, equipping believers for the work of the ministry? If so, how?

_____

_____

_____

If any one of those conditions was not met, then the vision or dream must be disregarded.

◇ What is God's attitude toward people who prophesy false dreams, leading people to error? (Jer. 23:32)

_____

_____

_____

◇ How does Scripture contrast the faithfulness of God's Word (Jer. 23:28–29) with words of false dreamers (23:30–32)?

_____

_____

_____

◇ What kind of things does 1 Thessalonians 5:21 say to test? What should we tightly hold on to? What should we avoid? (v. 22)

_____

_____

_____

◇ Is it possible to test a dream or vision without quenching the Spirit or despising prophecies? How? (See 1 Thess. 5:19, 20.)

_____

_____

_____

◇ 1 John 4:1 is the classic passage on testing truth. What does this verse say? Why is it important to do this?

_____

_____

Just as there were false prophets in the Old Testament who claimed to speak from the premise of a God-given dream, but in fact had not received such a dream, so there have been false prophets in every age since. There are false prophets today who claim to speak for God but in reality seek to lead people away from Him. God says to beware of them: "Beware of false prophets, who come to you in sheep's clothing, but inwardly they are ravenous wolves" (Matt. 7:15).

◇ Read Matthew 7:16–20. Write down the way in which we may detect or identify false prophets.

_____

_____

_____

◇ What is meant by "Therefore by their fruits you will know them"? (v. 20)

_____

_____

_____

FAITH ALIVE

Review a dream or vision of a person in the Bible you studied. As a practice exercise, use the scriptures and guidelines taught in this section to "test" the vision/dream. Determine to go through a similar procedure whenever you hear of a dream or vision that needs to be evaluated.

MAINTAIN BALANCE

Even though dreams or visions may truly be from God, it is important to again emphasize that the Scriptures do not ascribe special sacredness to dreams or visions in general. There is no set pattern of the type or variety of dreams in the Bible; neither is there a recommended "method" of interpretation through which we can seek guidance from them for our lives. The Bible simply affirms that on certain specific occasions God has chosen to make

His will known through prophetic dreams and visions. We are wise to acknowledge that fact and embrace them when God sends them.

Turn to Genesis 40:8 again. No matter what the situation, to whom does the interpretation of dreams and visions belong?

◇ The apostle Paul (who wrote much of the doctrine of the New Testament) said, "I was not disobedient to the heavenly vision" (Acts 26:19). How was his obedience to the vision God gave him demonstrated in his actions? (v. 20)

_____

_____

_____

_____

_____

Charles Spurgeon made a stunning declaration on the subject of spiritual balance: *"We must take care that we do not neglect heavenly monitions through fear of being considered visionary; we must not be staggered even by the dread of being styled fanatical or out of our minds. For to stifle a thought from God is no small sin."*

◇ Do you agree with Spurgeon? What are your thoughts?

_____

_____

_____

_____

_____

FAITH ALIVE

Name any cases you know of when people received a dream they believed to be from God, obeyed its direction, and experienced its fulfillment.

If you believe God has sent a dream to you, note how these verses can guide your response: 1 Thessalonians 5:8, 11–13, 16–22; 1 Corinthians 13.

DARE TO IMPART HOPE

Being a person of vision inspires hope in others. The prophet Ezekiel, himself a captive in Babylon, saw visions of God that flooded his heart with faith and gave him a message of hope for his fellow captives (Ezek. 1:1). Captivity, oppression, and slavery are among the most depressing conditions ever inflicted upon humankind. Yet, lifted by God's promise of deliverance made known in visions to Ezekiel, his people were able to endure their long and arduous trial.

DARE TO DREAM BIG

When Scripture said, "Joseph had a dream" in Genesis 37:5, it used words in the Hebrew that mean "to bind firmly." Joseph became *firmly bound up* in the dream that God had given him. Dreams that are from God are spiritual experiences that root deep in our hearts, never to be forgotten.

"Joseph had a dream," but perhaps we could more accurately say that the *dream had Joseph!* He held to the dream God gave him for his life. It kept him through everything he experienced. He was restrained from sin, redeemed from sorrow, and restored to honor by holding on to the dreams from God.

Let these five guidelines from Joseph's life inspire you to receive and hold on to *your* God-given dream:

1. Receive God's promise with childlike faith (Gen. 37:5–10)
2. Make the best of bad situations (39:4, 21)
3. Stand with integrity in trials and temptations (39:9)
4. Walk in humility before God and others (41:14–57)
5. See everything in life from God's perspective (45:7—50:20)

CONCLUSION

Biblical visionaries were people of intelligence and action, and they all had one thing in common: they were willing to wait for the Lord to speak to them. The prophet Habakkuk said it clearly: "I will stand my watch and set myself on the rampart, and watch to see what He will say to me, and what I will answer when I am corrected" (Hab. 2:1).

Do you want to be a person of vision? Stay in the Word of God. Listen to God's voice. Be open to the Holy Spirit. Be obedient to the "heavenly vision" God has given you. Receive it in faith as you follow His living Word.

FAITH ALIVE

Spend some time quietly before the Lord, actively seeking to hear His voice. What is the vision or dream God has given you? Has all of it been realized? Do you sense there is more? Write down what the Lord speaks to you.

Step out to be a leader of vision. Let God pour His dream into your heart and fill you with faith for its full realization.

Endnotes

[1] Leighton Ford, *Transforming Leadership* (Downer's Grove, IL: InterVarsity Press, 1991), 37.

[2] Ibid.

[3] Bill Hybels, *Descending into Greatness* (Grand Rapids, MI: Zondervan Publishing House, 1993), 16–17. Used by permission.

[4] *Nelson's New Illustrated Bible Dictionary*, Ronald F. Youngblood, General Editor. (Nashville, TN: Thomas Nelson Publishers, 1995), 846, "Miracles."

[5] *Hayford's Bible Handbook*, Jack W. Hayford, General Editor. (Nashville, TN: Thomas Nelson Publishers, 1995), 760, "Signs."

[6] *Hayford's Bible Handbook*, Jack W. Hayford, General Editor. (Nashville, TN: Thomas Nelson Publishers, 1995), 787, "Visions."

NOTES

NOTES

NOTES

NOTES

NOTES

NOTES

NOTES

NOTES

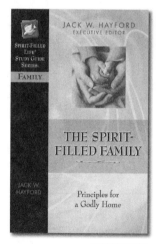